Immanence:

Selected, Collected Poems, Volume One,

1967-1988

James Howard Trott

Oak and Yew Press
Philadelphia

I0197212

OAK AND YEW
PRESS

Immanence:

Selected, Collected Poems, Volume One,

1967-1988

James Howard Trott

First printing

Oak and Yew Press
6705 North Eleventh Street
Philadelphia, PA 19126

ACKNOWLEDGEMENT

A number of the poems in this volume were first published in periodicals. A more specific accounting is included as an appendix. But it is appropriate to open this volume by extending grateful appreciation to the editors and poetry editors of these publications: *Christianity and Literature* (quarterly of the Conference on Christianity and Literature); *Cornerstone Magazine* (publication of Jesus People USA, Chicago); *New Horizons* (publication of the Orthodox Presbyterian Church, Philadelphia); *New Hope International* (special appreciation to Editor Gerald England, Hyde, England); *The Banner* (publication of the Christian Reformed Church, Grand Rapids); *Symphony* (Bemerton Press, Wembley, Middlesex, England), *Wellspring* (poetry quarterly, Menlo Park, California); *Plains Poetry Journal* (special appreciation to stalwart editor Jane Greer, Bismarck, ND); *Chronicles*; *Time of Singing* (Poetry Magazine of High Street Community Church, Conneaut Lake, PA); "Porch Swing Rhyme," former poetry column of The Society of Christian Poets, Van Buren, Arkansas; *Mythos*; "New Life News" and "Actstoo," newsletters of New Life Churches Jenkintown and Glenside, PA.

CONTENTS

IMMINENCE

The woods are still with waiting.
Noises of leaves and fleeing birds
Have passed.
Even the autumn furor of squirrels
Has subsided,
As they initiate snug mysteries,
Solitary meditations of hibernation.
These are the last few days of fall,
Most numinous.

Early days of thaw held promise.
Though bare as these first freezes,
Spring inclined toward life.
This field of woods promises nothing,
It forebodes.
Empty it is vibrant
With something foreign.

Perhaps it is silence,
Stealing beyond the ear,
Perhaps stillness,
Sentinel throughout the woodlot.

Only a tiny black and white woodpecker
Flits near invisible from high branch to bole,
Dropping a rising, piping note,
Thin against the imminence of winter,
Thinner still against the imminence.

OLYMPIC FINISH LINE

Running barefoot, ankles flexing roots, rocks,
The African sails along bright ridges,
Brown-bronze flash of thighs and calves
Pump primitively toward some dark goal.

Jogging among American suburbs, over
      asphalt,
Cars' antennae sensitive to his name,
Carelessly dressed against plutocracy,
The pink-tan, bearded contender pushes
      beyond.

Striders in Sweden, golden-haired ascetics
Along the streets of suicidal hedonists;
Sharp-featured Indians at Central American
      heights
Strengthening lungs and hearts in mile-high
      sacrifice;
Sinewed Gaulic competitors among slow
      existentialists;
Hide-minded Soviets for the glory of the
      proletariat,
For Russia, perhaps, for something censor-
      banned as well;
And the stiff limbs in the evening for stiff-
      lipped heroes
On the island where heroism is the religion,
Join with the swollen-jointed, broad-voiced,
Broad-shouldered athletes of broad antipodean
      reaches
In mysteriously similar sufferings:

Strident silence of all the racing heterogeny
Across the earth beyond each other's earshot.

Yet, when the pistol cracks, piston thighs
Hurtle gather-breathed celebrants
From attitudes of politics and self,
Crush every intention but that - the finish.
Amidst hurled discus, javelin, hammer,
Flying seemed eternities,
Times are shortened, times remade;
Teams with tears triumph in exhaustion:
Then those elect are one,
Tearing walls and curtains between them,
None unfamiliar to another,
Become comrades in deep bonds.

Some say athletics is the means to world peace
Despite international bloodshed and Olympic
        strife.
Others argue a marathon for all
Tribes, tongues, and nations, finishing in
        Olympus.

AS...SO

As the shark's bite tears flesh,
Cripples the water traveler,
Spilling the blood that frenzies
The shark to final attack,
So does God's grace halt,
Alarm and disable me
Before I am availed

Of grace in gaping measure.

As the slug's trail,
No wider than he,
But wide enough,
Smooths the way of snailing creature,
So falls the mercy of God
Beneath my feet at every step,
Providing the narrow way
Which lines my crawling life.

As the cloud of kings,
Monarchs, butterflies, cross
(To them) unknown reaches,
       continents,
Precisely, year upon year,
So do we, God's children,
Together home toward the unseen
Rest and fruitful place,
Grounds of our everlasting swarming.

ELUSIVITY

Certain species of woodpecker peck wood.
Others do not, nomenclature notwithstanding.
Rapid tappings across a woodlot
May be sounds of the former foraging,
But early birds or late occupy themselves
       variously,
Not always catching worms or grubs.
The tattoo may be territorial,
Or excavation of a nest.

It is hard labor getting to the bottom
Of the acts of creation;
Flickers, sapsuckers, hairy and pileated,
Birds of a feather go their diverse ways,
Finding beneath bark or in deeper wood,
Young or ancient, their sustenance.
Those which are true to their name
And happen to be hunting,
Bore unerringly at the right spot,
Pecking but the wood woodpeckers should
    To find their living food.

THE FIRM WARP

The fixed grid of universal lines,
Limits, bars, encloses
The free flow of spirit,
Life and thought: Time, space, mortality
Twisted tight like rigid rungs,
Ring like, clang like steel
Against warm human strivings.
Yet when the ever dipping thread
Of our brief life, the back and forth
One-pieced pliant woof is sent
By the hand of a skillful weaver,
We become against the warp a weft,
A woven fabric fit for use
In halls of a looming kingdom.

I WAS LOST

I was lost, diapered, blanketed,
Behind bars, without knowledge or strength,
Until my mother came with overflowing
      breasts.

I was lost, listless, in my own backyard,
Waiting without motivation or direction,
When my father came home at end of day.

I was lost, lonely, mindless in my malaise,
Elbows on knees, eyes dull blind,
Until, chores done my brother came out to play.

Though able, strong, and together, we were lost
Amidst fallen branches in dark woods
Until we were found by the hard searching
      path.

    I was lost
    But now I'm found.

TWO LOVERS

    This strange flesh which lingers near me
    Startles meditation to unseemly flight
    Weighs upon my finer motives,
    Anchors me to bed, to night.

    This strange soul possesses me,
    Turns my head from solid tasks;

Stays hands, feet from simple labors,
Enlightens little, too much asks.

This dull flesh is heir to folly,
Sin, sickness, and ugly age --
Wintry drafts which melt my candle,
Keep clear light from any page.

This fantastic soul's thin musings,
Dire constraints, unearthly rants
When I'm armed for mortal doings,
Strangle striving, disrupt dance.

These two lovers joined unwilling,
Often wanting here to part;
Teaching patience to each other,
Will rejoice with but one heart.

SALOME

You the epitome of Thomas' bait
With long legs girlish danced
Deadly for besotten father-step.
Herodias, your mother, reeling in angry,
Your lips triple-tined,
That booty dredged from dungeon floor,
Dark deep where misty-eyed
Last prophet long languished.
The head upon the platter
Was perhaps the only there
Not turned by long-legged dance,
A simple guerdon, girlish request,

The bleeding head of God's own emissary
Served up like a boar's, last course.
Perhaps those pretty legs long-trembled,
Lips paled at enormity of catch.
So struck bait is simply sacrificed,
Torn from the triple-tines, devoured --
Unless kneeling on short knees
You offered lips to that great catch,
Which yours presaged --
Bait, himself, pierced, able
To free from barbs and the long dance.

THE ROSE WEEVIL

Will weevil poets all thy buds consume?
Contumacy sweet galled by contumacy
      hellbent?
Well spent would be pure poison strewn;
Poor tunes and feeding teach such to repent.
Thy leaves they wound when petals they can't
      get,
Regret not hindering thine inward flow,
The slow bleeding of leaves' red pigments set
To fuse through narrow ways into thy blow.
Why not impale them on lawful thorns?
The sharp horn's point, dull creatures straying,
Turns all ways. Why unenforced against these
      scorns;
Insects warned not, though on thee preying?
I am such, on thee batten, fatten oft intent on
      evil.

Sharon's rose strangest grows: blossoms in a
    weevil.

FOUR ISAACS

Two Isaacs climbed two hilltops where one
    lived; one died.
Two sole sons two fateful mornings each on a
    mountainside.
Laughing mothers left behind them, neither
    guessed his end.
Two companions brought the tales back: a
    father, a friend.
The ancient father heard approved his sacrifice
    of love;
The modern Isaac's friend, Lord, heard thunder
    roll above.
Abraham saw a horn-hung ram, given for his
    son;
Eddie Lord saw his friend struck down, boy
    and beast as one.
The man stood by an altar, laid son on wood
    and stone;
The boy who rode behind his friend hurried
    back alone.
In his son, longed-for child, Abraham set great
    store ;
As Isaac Postill's life stopped short, so the
    name he bore.
The first lay down a sacrifice beneath his
    father's knife;

The latter drew lightning in the summer of his
     life.

The first Isaac died old, blessings gave his son;
The other died near mountain home, lost to
     everyone:
To mother from a distant isle, sisters
     unsorrowed 'til then;
To his father -- Isaac, also -- two laughters
     shared one end.
Near Abraham's hill hanged on post another
     sole son cried:
"It is finished. " As death struck, there death's
     power died.
Soon the old bones in Israel, these newer
     bones, our own
Shall rise and Jesus' joy transform the whole
     creation's groan
Into cries of understanding, recognition, there
     hereafter
Four Isaacs may embrace in joy: All Isaacs shall
     mean laughter.

TO FINISH AND TO FINISH WELL

I often wish my work were done,
My record closed on great coups won,
That my spent labors, taxings, tuition
Were ended, returned in full fruition.

This longing lengthens my mazed retracing,
My backward planning, past facts facing;

If only this or that effort I'd made,
Perhaps that hastened, this delayed.

Air castles behind as well as before me
Are peopled with sirens who say they'd adore
     me
To signify, to make my mark,
Leave a lingering light when I enter dark.

Were kindred thoughts in Gethsemane
     spoken?
What did "let this cup pass away" betoken --
Perhaps a longing for rewards begun?
How strange he added, "Thy will be done."

How nice to have rested on healings, raisings,
To bask in mankind's grateful praisings,
But no, his accomplishments all diminished
Until he last-gasped, "It is finished"!

TASKS

The other night I shook my boy,
With "Time to go potty, son."
It is my task to awaken him
To this small step toward manhood.
He quickly rose and stumbled through the
     light
Toward learning and the bathroom.
After his task I patted his head,
Wishing him good night.
Eyes still squenched nearly shut,

He made his way out , trailing back,
But swaying at the door, he turned,
Returned, and pursed his lips,
Offering a kiss, no duty, but free.
May I so love and honor him
Who taught my tasks to me.

MAN EMBARRASSED

I saw a man embarrassed
By the age of the woman on his arm,
(His mother, grandmother, mother-in-law?)
He hurried toward the nursing home doors,
In order to be relieved of her.

A man embarrassed
By age on his arm
Hurried toward the home
To be relieved of her.

Man embarrassed by age,
Hurried home
To be relieved.

Man, embarrassed, age,
Hurry, relieved.

Embarrassed?

REACH ME

Reach me, Oh Lord,
Behind the drawn down shades of my
      mountains,
In dreary depths of my sighing seas,
As far as earnest east from wistful west,
Reach thou me.

Reach me, Oh Lord,
Floating amidst corpuscular moments of time,
Wandering labyrinthine tunneled thought,
Wracked and fluttering far-flung by winds of
      passion,
Reach thou me.

Reach me, Oh Lord,
Worm away the gourd that succours me from
      thee,
Tornado my tabernacles, consume my Baal-
      built altars,
Lead me into alien spaces where your light
      unhindered
May shine upon my startled head -- there reach
      me,
Oh, Lord -- cause me to reach toward thee.

REVERIE

Fingers moving over strings fascinate,
And flames of fire.
Stars far above our reach and feel

Fill us with mute awe.

The mind no longer races,
Struggles of soul are stilled,
We look, we watch, we wait
Without anxiety of waiting.

Whether fingers guide a needle
Or conjure a melody,
Whether flame be campfire or candle
(The star always a star)
We gaze and rest, our beings fixed
For a moment on an object.

Something in us, mind, soul, or body
Finds such things gracious,
Silent partner, submits
To being led in quiet dance.

This in an old word is reverie
                    . . . Reverence.
Shall we somewhere rest and gaze
Upon fingers, flame, or star
In endless fascination?

SESSALG DERORRIM NI NAM EHT

The man in mirrored glasses walked demented,
Hidden in the noon-day sun.
Twin lenses flashed a code,
Some ancient, obscure heliography.

Beneath the looking glasses
Snow-white teeth froze a smile, fading not,
Prophetic glory reflecting
Blinding in-sight.

I looked the striding in the face
But for a moment, saw myself there
In glass, under glass, friends and nation
Reflected darkly.

What secret malice preened
Itself behind lenses
Through which one might see
Others seeing but oneself?

In twin mirrors facing one another
One may see both, myriad,
In a moment diminish.
Infinity flashes each to each.

We stand before single spectacles
To balm pride, hair, or body,
To review time's passages,
But these lenses faced none, themselves.

Bright lenses facing outward told no tale,
Hinted not, yet cried some great
Emptiness behind, blackened mirrorback,
Pitch or paint; backward eyes if any.

When men in mirrored glasses meet
In flashing dual reciprocation,

There in tense reflections
Who can bare their eyes to see?

WEAPONRY

Some people's lives are canister,
Some people's cannon ball.
Some people's lives are rifle fire,
Some people's misfires all.
Some people must muzzle load,
Some fire like automatics,
Some launch long range missiles,
Others hurl sharp sticks.
Comparisons of range and power,
Their contrasting ballistics
May sometimes be of interest
To students armed with statistics;
But after the shooting stops,
The question will be framed,
Not how loaded, how big, how loud,
But which way each was aimed.

RELATIVITY

What though the world be God's subjective
        thought,
A mote on his eyelash he made of was-not?
Relative to God the distinction is small
Whether the world exists or is idea all.
What God makes and what he thinks are one.
Strange tidings though it be to some,

What we think and make are distinguished
      wide;
True doggerel does dreamed poem deride;
Consideration spends riches never made;
Matter over mind holds out bills unpaid.
Think what we will, world-wide needle's eye
We cannot pass; neither wealthy nor sly.
Not the best assessment overrides our station:
We live and have being but in relation
To a wide world and world making power.
Though some may reign, arraign, arrange one
      hour,
No weather-man holds back the falling rain
      ringing
On man's fallen work, with so few scions
      springing.
We tender few acts in our thoughtful proclivity
Down near the bottom of the law of relativity.

NO RAIN

No Rain
They predicted and fair tomorrow,
Upon which sanguine prophecy
Some based their fair-weather plans
(Although the much abused shamans
Have only a 30 percent chance of being
right,
And we their devotees know it.)
When the storm boiled up in the north,
A line of shadow stealing like some thief
Across the clouds, sunlight faded,

Yet we studiously labored to ignore it.
Not until the rain burst
In dense, undeniable, inescapable showers
Did we stop our work, all unprepared.
But will it be fair tomorrow?

THIS LITTLE LIGHT OF MINE

I cannot show it here
Nor spend it on now's moment.
It's saved for when the hour is reached
Where ambiguity is breached
. . .For when I'm sure.

I once was told I carried it
Upon my person heaven-sent,
Then cautioned I should use it well
To light my path away from hell
. . .If I could keep it lit.

But I have yet to find a place
Wherein I dared to burn it bright.
Those yet have been so very dark,
And I have known no certain mark
. . .Sure spark in any face.

Some day my flame will shine
When there is no more night.
Or must I take the awful chance
And in the darkness make it dance
. . .This little light of mine?

WHAT HEARTY PRESENCE

What hearty presence beats at man's most
      inward part?
Mind's musty mutterings grow mum,
Flimsy feelings flow and fly away --
This for them a conundrum.

Mind logically arranged, constrained, knows
      not
Heart-leap, heart-break, or heart's ease.
Emotions, fevered, effervescent, fail to plumb
Heart's flow, heart's tides and seas.

Life's true labors are no syllogisms, squares,
Nor loves thrills of nerves or sense.
Man's heart holds sway, what rules him rules
      there.
Mind and emotion bear their offerings thence.

WHO LEAPS FROM BRIDGES

Who leaps from bridges arching floods
Dives to darkened dreams.
Crumbling, ugly though they be,
Bridges are for crossings.
Prescience perhaps, or post-science,
Of throngs thrusting, flocks herded
Between two posts over rude floods
Drive the desperate to do. . .
Or is it sudden looming dreads
On misty nights when so few pass

That all at once dim spans may end?
These or deeper knowing yet
The crossed may ford on dying visions,
Of what one is, what one may be, do,
Pipe the unembattled, fooled,
To leap the rail to unseen certain,
With muffled cry heard around the world.

PREDESTINATION

The latent radiance of the shadows;
The brightness building in cracks of the world;
The secret rain in innocent clouds;
Green May shoots from patches of mud:
Predestination.

To talk long and loud of garden botany,
Rainfall in weather and fraction of inches,
Spotlight, searchlight, flashlight and daylight,
Requires no humility, nothing faith.
Predestination: not that life can account for
        life,
But that darkness shall blaze.

PACE

I would pace my life with even stride
Or stretch my legs one friend beside ,
So to find welcome at each open gate ,
Full well   received   nor   tarrying late .

I would not rush early wealth to find ,
Nor too soon fill this vault of mind ,
Nor memory load with myriad pleasures
Nor hearty hall with hasty treasures .

I would not scale the peaks too soon :
A morning zenith means a fading noon .
Lead me always by thyself good friend
That my slow profit but you may spend .

CHRISTMAS LABORS

A wistful winebibber sat in the wide foyer
Wearing his seasonal red suit and hot whiskers
Processing a line of children yet more cynical
Than last year's horrible crop.
Echoing through the broad ethers of the
        complex,
While herds of hasty shoppers galloped below,
Hung Christmas music, adoration mixed with
        inanity.
As a famous cult choir rendered Handel's
        Hallelujah,
Santa Claus (Wonderful Counselor)
Took another boy upon his knee (Almighty
        God)
And promised him what he wanted
        (Everlasting Father)
If he would be good and (Prince of Peace)
Concluded half-heartedly, "Ho, ho, Merry
        Christmas."
The child climbed down, not much impressed.

The vinegar-breathed man wiped his forehead
    on a cotton cuff
And asked himself if anyone ever suffered so
    unjustly.

MARCH FRUIT

The bitterness of winter
Lingers on our tongues,
But it is early March
And the maple tree, still leafless,
Has brought forth hanging fruit,
Fruit of promise.
The boy-broken branches
Have begun to flow with sap
Night- frozen in white, dripping banners.
We pick them, these jewels
Of substantial tree's blood.
We suck their sweet kisses
Which make us thankful for wounds,
This assurance of coming spring.

SHADOWS RUNNING TOWARD THE LIGHT

Down, down came the snow
In gathered clumps,
Hindered only by its clumsy shapes
Dropping into windless evening,
But as we watched them
In the reflected light
Of their fallen history

And in the great tent
Of the street lamp,
We saw something else:
Gray phantoms, mouse ghosts
Ran steadily from our front porch
Across the intersection
And from all directions
Impelled toward the lamppost.
Our eyes strained to hold
The three motions at once:
The snow vertically descending,
The golden light radiating,
And across the silent whiteness
The hurtling shadows converging
Like small snow souls
Drawn to the tabernacled source --
Shadows running toward the light.

TILL THE EARTH

"Till the earth out of which you were taken,"
Cloud-clapping words must have mud-man
    shaken,
Set clay-clapped, dirty-eared Adam quaking.

Plow up the stuff of which you were made,
Thorn-thick, flesh-tearing, fang-betrayed.
No more hiding in garden shade.

Cut the pelt of the innocent earth,
Poor brother once in rich garden mirth
That you sin-soiled so soon after birth.

Dig! Fashion hoes, shovels, rakes.
Raise what your mote-eyed partner bakes.
Groan with creation in briars and brakes.

Work the earth, pain-borne family and food,
Your meager lot 'til Cain-shed blood
Cries out from the ground, as all earth should.

With his fingers dusty (flesh dust still)
A man sowed forgiveness, planted on hill,
Tilled new life into earth a new earth until.

GOD'S TEMPERAMENT?

Phlegmatic! His judgment falls so slow.
Melancholy! He suffered, sorrows so.
Choleric! How angry he has been!
Sanguine. His blood's excess --
    Covers so much sin!

SECOND STORY MAN

Jesus is a second story man.
When they hung him, they hung him high,
For breaking in when all were asleep,
For having no alibi.

Jesus is a second story man.
Climbed up the narrow way,
Shined his light through tiny cracks

Before the break of day.

Jesus is a second story man,
He came and knocked at the door.
By the time you were armed to open up,
He was on the second floor.

Jesus is a second story man,
Came down the whole long way --
From his high place to this low dive,
Holed up in a house of clay.

Jesus is a second story man
The goniff between two thieves.
He broke out and is coming back
To steal off whomever believes.

LIKE A LOVER'S LOVE

Like a lover's love, forceful, passionate,
        demanding,
His love would be horrible if I could not
        return it.
He would be brutal, rapist, cruel ravager.
(Love like that is no love)
His is lover's, makes me love him back.
Not sweet, except by exception,
(Love that is only sweet is no love)
In the small times of candy and flowers.
His love is awesome by and large,
Jealous, asking, drawing, taking all,
Like a lover's love.

THE CREED/THE HERETIC

(antiphonal)
    Molecular in generation, worship one
    Through aeonic forms and stages now
        become
(unison)
    Highest creature on the earth,
    Though mayhem mark his life and birth,
    A holy son.

(antiphonal)
    From a gram of ninety-second comes a flash:
    Energy from matter rages, fire from ash.
(unison)
    Miracle to preach to nations,
    Threatening death bright revelation --
    Adam smash.

(antiphonal)
    Truth exists in what is proven, cogito ergo
        sum
    All there is we'll one day know, let that day
        come.
(unison)
    Trust your mind, trust no others,
    Data banks are our true brothers,
    Hymns they hum.

(antiphonal)
    Urges rule us in all matters, live and eat
    Biological our motives, glands secrete.

(unison)
  Though we practice sublimation
  All mankind of every nation
   Is in heat.

(antiphonal)
  Empty gods and spirits taunt us on our beds.
  Outworn myths these are that haunt us, skins
        to shed.
(unison)
  Man is matter, life is motion,
  Spirit is a bygone notion,
  Kill it dead.

(antiphonal)
  Every man is but a product, mutants few,
  Bits of endless generations, sum in you.
(unison)
  Common the equations of us all . . .

(lone voice)
  Yet first I doubt, then tip the scale and fall
  At Heaven's feet , a heretic. Adieu!

MUSHROOM HUNTING

  In wet woods of early fall
  Still rain came down
  Urging tenuous leaves toward the
        inevitable;
  But having no sense or history,
  They clung as though life lasts.

I knew better and garnered irretrievable
Moments of time from the fading season,
Hunted mushrooms, my excuse.

Two fungi I found, Amanita and
    Strobilomyces,
Virosa and floccopus, respectively:
The former deadly, the latter edible.
There amidst the dripping trees,
The clean white Death Angel shone
In an angle of light,
While only the warty brown Old Man of the
    Woods,
Broken flesh flushing crimson,
Would prove savoury.
To make good my excuse I picked the latter
Before it was hidden in fallen leaves.

MARCH HAWK

A March Hawk skudded the long gray
    wind,
Silent, swift before its pursuers,
Somber, almost black between dim sky and
    bonestruck trees.
Three deaths lingered in my mind,
Three swift passages in one week
Marshaled there behind the hawk
I saw from the ridge of my friends' roof.
Theirs two deaths: their ebullient springer
And an unborn nephew-niece.
Such an excess of sorrow as they knew

For the creature promising less
Was perhaps meant to suffice for that
Immortal kin-child they never met.
First in time and expectation, third gone,
An eighty-five-year-old brother, mine,
In high hospital there beyond the trees
Within my sight, yet no more, and I
Prognosticated recovery, predilected
      roofing,
Did not say farewell to him
Whose faring could but be well.
The hawk moved at great speed, effortless,
Lifting great wings only to sail.
Not even two crows attracted by strident
      mourning
Could catch the raptor,
Gliding almost inevitable across morning
Before inevitable spring.
Leaving the dead to bury their dead,
The hawk hurried on toward Easter.

THE SCHOOL OF REALISM

Going among the realists
We were abruptly reminded
By an officious steward
Not to point or gesture
Near the canvases.
We did not ascertain
The limits of their resurrected,
Taboo glory in inches.
Assumedly the chance touch

Of an unwashed human finger
Might in one moment
Do more damage than
Sixty years of criticism,
Slashing them to abstract ribbons.
The real may not touch
Even realists' art.

OLD CURSES

'In the sweat of your brow
You shall bring forth your bread'
Was old when Adam was sod;
Was spoken when he and all mankind
Were a glimmer in the eye of God.
The earth shall bring forth thistles, as well,
Long before earth was, was said;
Before there were fields or plows or trees
Thorns circled about God's head.
'Pain you shall have in childbirth'
A precursor knew before Eve.
Before there were trees or fruit or snakes,
God's issue took pains to achieve.
'You shall want to rule and be overruled'
Was laid out before mates were made,
In the mystery of the echoing void
Coinherent exchanges were played.
'An enmity be between you' --
Before high stars flamed and fell;
'You shall bruise his heel and he your head'
-- From the first so cursed was hell.

James Howard Trott

ODE ON HIS FIDDLING
for Richard Wyatt*

A poor song I dight thee,
An ode scarce worth a pin.
How can a poet's pen pretend
To play to a violin?
Yet of thee 'tis said, alas,
Thou didst trade the latter
Forever for the former.
So much the Muse left sadder.
For music is the Muse's own,
Despite what poets disburse.
Often a man will escape from words
With a tune -- rare the reverse.
Thy fiddling was powerful potent,
So the whispering ghosts relate,
Until thou settedst thine fiddle down,
Damming that musical spate.
The reason for thy precipitate act,
The sad spheres vibrate still,
(Unless it be but jealously
Ground from flyblown rumor mill).
Yet let it never be said of thee
Thy playing was weak nor dry
Nor for all your urge to empower it
It would not harm a fly.

*(Richard studied the violin diligently,
practicing in his attic until one day he was
completely discouraged by a singular event:
As he practiced a fly fell dead upon his
strings. He never played again.)*

OTHER PEOPLE'S WINDOWS

Other people's windows are not for my
    eyes,
Others' lives not my own.
Other people's houses are castles closed
With moats filled, hedges grown.

Though they have no curtains,
Though they've open hearts,
Though they fly flags of peace
And practice peaceful arts,

Though the lights shine out from them,
And words ring sweet,
Though they may invite me in,
Serve good wine and meat --

Other people's windows are not for my
    eyes.
Others' names and fates not for me to
    prize.
Other people's wakings and others' sleep
Are for other people and God to keep.

A SCARLET THREAD

A scarlet thread flowed down a head from
    under a crown, out a rude bed;
Through Abel's wounds wound, called out
    from the ground, first murderer found;

To a small hand extended, which Tamar's
      shame ended, whom Judah offended;
Through wilderness wended, willing offering
      lended, with dark linen blended
To adorn courts inner and outer for sinner,
      sewed seamstress and skinner.
The thread through the tent with other hues
      blent, through the ephod, too, went;
Other clothes for the priest: girdle, breastplate,
      eyes' feast, robe, not least,
Were likewise shot through amidst gold,
      purple, blue, with sure scarlet hue,
Pomegranate-embroidered with bells,
      reconnoitered if the high priest loitered,
Both fruit red-celled and the border gold-
      belled in the Holy Place knelled.
Like a wine-soaked cloth, spun scarlet swathed
      shone tabled bread soft;
Scarlet Rahab's ties, spoken token of spies
      saved the sinner despised;
Her household as well, drawn from Jericho's
      hell, on the thin thread tell.
Then a king came, Saul; girls lamented his fall,
      who in scarlet decked all;
David's son wrote: hear, a good wife won't fear
      when snow-time is near
For her family's dressed in scarlet, the best;
      at fierce weather jest.
(Not only for sewing was that king's going
      after scarlet smile glowing.)
Stark Isaiah, also, saw scarlet turn snow,
      God scours men so;

The Lamenter gave warning, who in scarlet go
    scorning hug dunghills by morning;
Daniel, clean prayer, lion-hearted sooth-sayer,
    received of one payer
Scarlet clothes, gold chains, for God-given
    pains, third king's realm and reins;
Nahum said oppressors would meet scarlet
    dressers, worms turned to aggressors,
With shields flaming red, fiery chariots torch-
    led making trees shake in dread.
Yet more ready no wise, Israel angry despised
    one strangely disguised
With bruised reed sceptre, scarlet-robed
    preceptor; Roman guards were adepter,
Bid that lashed back thread joined others bled
    from limbs, side, head;
Doves', cattle's, lambs' -- bulls', calves', rams':
    pooled doom law-dammed
Flowed a scaffold flume to a stone-sealed tomb,
    where in deepest gloom,
By folded cloths sapped, around mystery
    wrapped,
. . . the scarlet thread snapped.

TRANSUBSTANTIATION

No pious cant can satisfy us hungry,
For mortal flesh staves off mortality
With broken flesh of grain and creature.
Flesh battens on flesh, not on spirit.
Manna-fed Israel woke hungry each day.
Dust lives on dust, in dust, out of dust

And blows as dust at last breath.
Exceptional Enoch, Elijah, and Jesu
Spiraled up divine wind leaving no mote.
Some envy them, but stomach mine
Groans homelier chords of practical
      philosophy
Wondering what they eat there.
(Food for thought, thought flying thin
Betwixt stuff of flesh and spirit.)
What might mortal innards do
With victuals sublime and viands?
Yet a more knotty digestive query,
What do immortal bowels with mortal
      aliments?
For angels ate with Abraham, dined, too,
      with Lot.
Direst disturbance: Christ, resurrected, fed
On half-baked bread and Galilean fishes.
What cataclysmic reception did those
Corruptible morsels find in incorruptible
      body?
Cant aside, phenomenal and noumenal met.
Some fundamental transubstantiation
      occurred.

NOTED GUESTS

Adam threw a party,
      it was at his father's place.
Eve adorned the cards with apples,
      they started quite a race.
For they have a reputation

for exotic things to eat,
Not to mention guests who gather
    from among the world's elite.
Superbia was there decked out
    in her latest royal gown;
Most everyone paid homage
    to her jewelry and crown.
Ira followed just behind,
    the two are very close -
She was drinking like a trooper
    and gave us all a dose.
Luxuria was driven, spoke
    of all she'd like to have.
She believes in scratching itches
    or at least applying salve.
Gula came early, said, "I'm
    simply famished, dear."
The drinks were on the house and
    "the chef is new I hear!"
Avaritia talked business, "
    What with all the kids to feed,
There's so little to fall back on
    in case of time of need."
Accidia was free that night,
    and thought she should relax,
"Life is such an awful ratrace,
    one needs a little pax."
Invidia rushed in, took
    notes on all the rest,
Saying, "Why have I such awful luck,
    don't I deserve the best?"
And all were well-accompanied,
    so it was a wondrous bash,

But when someone throws a party,
  someone's sure to crash.
The fame of that great feast
  spread further than you'd think:
Four guests arrived on horseback,
  not stopping for a drink.
One isn't safe any longer with
  the social graces gone!
Those rogues raised hell, scared everyone,
  and ruined the front lawn.
Then one last guest, a mystery, showed.
  We haven't heard to date
How he came to know young Adam,
  or why he came so late.

AN IMPRESSION

During a two day retreat from other
  responsibilities
My wife and I went to get acquainted again
Amidst the art works of the National Gallery,
Looking at the reflections in one another's
  minds.
There we saw a Rodin exhibit which declared
The difference between craft and art,
Between image and imagination.
In order to renew our visions,
We climbed up to the Renaissance and
  Impressionists,
Who, tending perhaps heretical, at least tended.
Leaving the museum we were surprised
To enter a Seurat landscape carelessly left out.

We returned to our car catching the white
       points,
Dabs of a lucid artist in our open, thirsty
       mouths.

A LOST OFFICE

In democratic frontier fury we threw off
       monarchy.
Rebels, said the king. We called it
       revolutionary,
Threw off unrepresented taxes, soldiers lodged
       in homes,
Threw off tyrant tea,
Yankee-doodled all things monarchical out of
       the land,
Speaking brave words: government of, by and
       for the people.

In doing so we bid adieu not only to England,
But to ages of European kings, queens and
Lords and ladies, knights and squires,
Powdered wigs, afternoon tea, Oxford,
       Cambridge,
Aristocratic blood and crown jewels,
Castles, dungeons, towers and poets laureate.

Few bemoan the divorce.
We lost, however, an office and institution
Which was loss indeed.
At the time of our departure the European
       monarchs, too,

Seem to have misplaced him, the voice of
      imbecilic truth
 Which every American must play for himself:
Lost office of court jester -- or fool.

ECHOES

The deaf do not hear,
Therefore do not speak.
Visual signals they send
Across crowds and in silent situations,
Where hearing we are handicapped.

Echo voices over sigh-high panoramas
Thrill the listening heart:
Mountain sends to mountain,
Deep to deep the small-stilled revelations;
There are no echoes on the plains.

The fault in you which most offends
The hearing, seeing mountain me
Is this you cry in greatest voice,
That I send back so echo clear.
Only the free from sin can forgive.

HOPE

Sells insurance for giant corporations,
Great headless bodies, twice blasphemous,
Giving profitable assurances
Of things only actuarially to happen,

And gambler's chances for governments,
Taking substance from the weakest
To fatten tyrannical servanthood,
Bloated heads devouring their bodies.
It furnishes, as well, a round syllable
Synonymous for wish, doubt, might have been.
But churches retain it, list it high
Among desirables, with faith and love,
As they kowtow to government, buy insurance,
And send weekend busloads to gambling
     resorts.
 I had almost forgotten hope meant other,
 Having groped my way into this dark vision
 In which it was but a distant glimmer,
 A sometimes seen promise of this tunnel's
     end,
 Until I tripped on some small rock,
 Bumped my head awake, and saw the blazing
     sun.

COURTESY

Omnipotence bowed gracious before
     infirmity,
Poisoned flesh teeming with a thousand ills,
Condescended to take up suffering stuff
Into golden arms, more than golden,
More than arms, feet, head, and heart,
Penultimate courtesy.

Tottering infirmity, finite churl
Commanded infinity to be born rude,

Compelled most rude rood to be borne,
Yet omnipotence bowed gracious before
      infirmity,
Far more than courteous.

Omnipotence dropped into arms infirm,
Set hope aside and hoped in hapless
To catch, wash, clothe and anoint,
Who fallen, stinking, and deluded
Wandered barely through held-back night.

And grace upon grace
Infirmity was let bow before omnipotence,
Last courtesy the greatest,
Omnipotence folded frail clothes,
Transformed infirm to faultless,
Reserving only sovereignty
That there might continue courtesy.

TENDER HAMMER

Tekton of Nazareth, how often watched your
      son
And learned of you, your skillful hammer
      swung
To drive the nail or split the stone?

Mason of Jerusalem, were you careful in the
      gloom
Gathering as you hewed the newmade tomb
Handmade of hammerstrokes for bone?

Smith of legions wielding your maul,
Did you at any time regret its ring and fall
Or swords and spears shaping in each shock?

Soldier on Golgotha, was it child's play
Driving spikes through flesh as though
      through clay?
Did ever your wide mallet pause or balk?

You who fitted ancient temple halls
Or thousand crosses sledged outside the walls
How much love was in your clamor?

Yet ask I one to take this, useless, rough,
And rain down blows with strength and skill
      enough
To re-form *me* beneath his tender hammer.

NO WONDER

    The men whose wives,
    Yea, mothers, too, whose daughters
    Are but afterbirths to their desires,
    Ought not to rock in such surprise
    When daughters treat their own likewise:

    Destroying the afterbirths of their desires
    As tissue without life or value.

    It takes some fortitude, a particular vision
    Alien to man and woman-kind
    To affirm and cherish your womb's fruit

When you yourself are destitute.

"C"- SECTION

They were professionals
Who fastened you cruciform,
Hardboiled wisemen
With their radio playing,
Yet what their hands did
Was so far out of their hands
They might as well have admitted it,
For the Father picked you out
While the world was *in utero*
To suffer that another might have life:
To come to the point
Where you needed him desperately
To help me know I did, too.
When that blade sliced your abdomen,
Blood mingled with water
And I knew there was a curse.
When that life came forth,
I knew the curse was lifted.

THE OTHER TOMB

Locked in a barely stable room,
Because there was no space in the tomb,
A paranoid band of retired fanatics,
Fearing the future, hid all in an attic.

The stone had sealed their expectations;

Old bread, sour wine, remnants, their rations.
They lingered under the city's bans,
Too much confused to make travel plans.

Well-embalmed in thorough despair
Against the pneumatic germ in the air,
Only a few let rot their gloom
At the woman's tale of an empty tomb.

That tomb's not empty, nor this one, either.
Better we'd died and heard of neither.
Thomas vowed not to die alive
Unless his own hand felt wounds five.

That tomb-room door remaining locked,
Jesus was with them! their dark death
   mocked,
Bidding Thomas come, his wounds to feel;
Touched his, deeper, doubt's sting to heal.

There a second resurrection occurred.
A vision-dead band of poor and absurd,
Fishermen, scoundrels, leaping up living,
Went out to wake other dead with forgiving.

THE BEST LAST

The best wine is usually first,
Youth, health, simple pleasures
Fade in the chaos of age,
Complexity, jaded sense, toward death.
Who is this disorderly wedding guest

Handling wine like water
And passing out the best last?
I know him, said Nathanael,
He saw me with spiritual eyes.
I knew him for miracle-worker,
But this mystery he spoke to me --
Greater miracles that I should see.
Yet I know him not, little at least,
Although I accompany him to this feast.
How, for instance, could things get better
Than this beginning at a wedding supper?
But I have heard dark hints and read
Of a worse end which we only dread.
Will he look then in his bitter cup,
Say the best wine's last brought up?

CONCERNING THE GODS

They say Thor hurled thunderbolts
With his bare hands,
But no record remains
Of one hurled in upon himself.

Poseidon rowled the flanks
Of the furious sea, sent
Crashing storms upon the helpless,
But never drowned himself.

No strange god regretted
The eternal curse of Sisyphus
And put everlasting hands
To stone of struggling mortal.

No Olympian anomaly
Unchained the torn Prometheus
To take his place
Beneath fierce mountain eagles.

What one stooped thunderstruck
Beneath his overwhelming flood
With hands bloodworn in labor,
His body eagle-torn?

MY HANDS

My right hand is my left hand's worst
        enemy.
For all the help it gives
My left receives but wounds.
Small solace when the right washes,
Wipes the blood away.
To be gently wrapped in sterile dressing
Makes no amends for clumsiness or
        treachery.

Adding insult to injury
My right's called dexterous,
But my left sinister --
Innuendo, false witness.

This south paw is foolish and forgetful.
It longs to leave its bandages,
To rise, assist again,
To hold the chisel, beam, or nail
Allowing the right to strike again.

Perhaps it will do so,
Forgiving too much,
Until my right hand learns
What my left hand has been doing.

SIN-BEARER

On a sensual sally into the old dump
Beyond the reservoir dam,
And out of sight of the farm,
I met another trespasser.
I was there foraging for fatal photo magazines
Bedraggled by water and time, moldy and
    forbidden
By a law no elements could erode from my
    heart.
The porcupine was there to eat
The bark from a few hardbitten trees,
Five or six survivors out there on the prairie.
The magazines were planted
In that place of rust and refuse
By neighbors or neighbor's hired men.
The trees were planted by the dam builder,
I guess, before I can remember.
I found magazines, feasted my eyes
On legs and breasts in faded ink,
On wrinkled pages mixing old truths and lies.
And under the burden of my hot guilt
I started back toward the farm
Startling the porcupine in tall grass.
He turned his back and bristled,

While I, enraged by fear on top of guilt,
Ran back to the dump for an adequate weapon
With which to judge the sin-heavy beast.
Returning I found him defensively crouched,
So, panting out my condemnation, I beat him,
Laid my blows on his back
Until it broke and he died.

THE MAN WHO SWEEPS OLNEY

The man who sweeps Olney smiled today,
The man who walks the gutters brushing
     rubbish away.
His face was creased distinctly, I saw him as I
     passed --
Who never wore a smile before -- may it not be
     his last.

Another stood beside him, one who must have
     caused
The unaccustomed mirth which on the rough
     face paused.
It was a young apprentice who held the broom
     instead
And will no doubt sweep Olney when the old
     man is dead.

OLNEY QUEEN

An empty sky
Is plastered across

The empty sign scaffold.

The gray pigeon
Wings flash down
Orange dawn.

The rusted-out tinwork
Apartments of the starlings
Discharge their workmen.

Smoke of coffee
Wavers over
Formica altars.

Crackling voices,
Hoarse shufflings,
Break our fast like prayers.

MOSQUITO

Lying in the welter of my blood she's dead,
Lawfully struck. Perhaps she'll haunt no more.
She took what carries life through me,
I took from her her creaturehood.

She wanted my best to raise her brood,
I wanted her life to save me pain,
Yet in that taste, her little gain,
She left my mind and memory food.

Something in me she thought good:
The blood of mine she saved I shed,

And though I slap until I'm sore,
She still flies, humming 'round my head

WHITEWASH

With the slapping of your brush you sprinkle,
      wash,
Splash, paint, pour lime over me.
I the crumbling earthen-walled vessel,
I the mouldering basement of your house.

With the shaking of your brush you sprinkle
          cleansing,
Caustic, cleansing, righteousness,
This foreign stuff which binds and covers,
Makes me shine, reflect the light I little did
          before.

With the aspergation of your brush you
          whitewash me,
Not to flash like sepulchres which stink inside,
But in thorough scouring power which robes
My heart and mind as much as outward parts.

With the wide stroke of your brush you
          whitewash me,
Changing the essential man to something pure,
Something new which suits your shining glory
          better
Though horribly you burn your hands, you
          whitewash me.

With the touches of your brush you whitewash
     me,
Turned from black to red to white, and though
They sprinkled you with none so gentle
     strokes,
Yet patiently and ever with your blood you
     sprinkle me.

BARBERSHOP QUARTET
I. THE BARBERSHOP

Outside the barbershop the pole spins on
In fascinating colors, red, white,
Heightening the seeing senses,
Lifting the eyes of passersby,
The sauntering male populace,
Needing, getting ready for,
Looking for a haircut.
Atop the pole an opaque globe,
Foggy crystal ball, dead eye, stares back.

Inside around the thrones,
Conversation spirals up,
Highflown rhetoric tossed to and fro
Encompasses all and everything.
Anecdotal observations pass old wisdom
To young hands, heads soon to be shorn.
The inner circle know themselves,
Are known by instinct, given way.
The old bucks, the grizzled talkers,
Incite the least to aspiration.
Before the mirror the half-revealed message

On the upright razor holder reads "sterile".

On the wall a calendar,
On the shelves a rainbow garden
Of scents and stimulants to catch
Helpless hungry beauty portrayed there.

But all of this may vary -- settings only,
Ever shifting: shops close, shops open,
Barbers come and barbers go,
Customers are a constant stream
In which even regulars are irregular.

Yet in the corner gray-leaved piles
Of magazines, the holy writ changes not,
Uniting brotherhoods in barbershops
Since Caesar was a little shaver.
Cars and sports, and guns and sex:
These the spirits of the well-groomed gods:
Speed and strength and blood and manhood.
And as for speed, it shall slow;
As for strength, it shall diminish;
And as for shedding blood, it shall end,
But lust lingers on to the grave.

And the brotherhood brooks no heresy,
Allows no apostasy.
No Sunday School boy may enter
Without paying homage to the calendar girl,
Reading the day's homily, doing his devotions
Among the appointed passages.
Should any try to shirk the obligations,
He can find no place to rest,

His eyes shifting from lock-littered floor
To porcelain fixture to fly-blown ceiling
To Barber's disapproving feet,
Until at last by way of mirror
Or out of the corner of his eye
He's yanked back to orthodoxy.
The hot-necked guilt of unbelief
Prepares his short hairs for the cutting,
The burn and the razor ready for such as him.

"Barber-us, Barber-us" the customers cry,
And the governing barber washes his lily
       hands.
Perhaps a low-toned comment as the youngster
Stumbles out into fresh conviction
Of cool air on his new-shaved neck,
Stumbles out mute, passing the next coming in.

"Crop, crop, crp" the scissors chant,
While the harvest falls haphazard
Not for threshing, but for burning.
Black, blonde, all shades of brunette,
Auburn and white, straight and curly,
No distinction, democracy at its best'
"Burrrrrrrrrrrrrnnnnnnnnnnnnnzzzzzzzzz"
The eastern clippers intone, mesmerize
The newcomer in the corner into the illusion
That he and the naked girl on the page
Are all alone this side of heaven.

The barberpole spins on, spins up,
With red for blood-letting,
From the days when razors were more frank

In their hypocrisy, two-edged,
And two-purposed - hair and health.
Razors and leeches, removing Samson's hair
And sucking out his vitality,
Well-matched trades behind one symbol.
And white - for what?
Purity? Sterile instruments? Or unspeakable,
The spilled seed in the corners of solitary
bedrooms. . .

Not quite unspeakable among the brotherhood,
Who may mention it in their jokes,
Stale cigar-breathed jokes, sops tossed to ears,
Which are owed a little burning
When eyes are allowed so much.

And the mirrors record all for posterity,
For the record, the infinite detail,
The procession, the repeated counter spin
Of boys, men and souls into defeat,
Well-attended defeat, well-supported defeat,
Defeat thoroughly enjoyed,
Which enjoyment is also delineated
In the flashing back and forth images
Which go on unending from mirror to mirror
Soul to soul, so that none may testify
I did not see it happen, not in me.

Every eye's corner sees the mirror's messages,
The complex angles up and down, side to side,
And out the window. Every eye sees itself
        momentarily,

In the uncomfortable moment of approving the
        shearing.
But the eyes are occupied otherwise as well.
The calendar girl's eyes say,
All this has some meaning, objectivity.

II. THE EYES HAVE IT

In the barbershop and at the hairdresser's
The brotherhood and sisterhood
Are separately in agreement --
The eyes have it.
All they are and all they desire
Receives impetus, assent and ardor
Through the eyes.
The nays are unintelligible and faint.
No man, no woman is so blind
As to vote the eyes for simple seeing.

III. CALENDAR GIRLS

The calendar girls walk along the sidewalks
Avoiding eyes like manholes with lids up,
Staring apertures full of possibility.
(You have to take a chance to get ahead)
The hollow hiss of hidden torrents
May barely reach their virgin ears.

But the phenomenal light reflected by
The surfaces of the solids of the beings
Which are they sends like messages

Into the black holes of the furtive watchers.
The truck drivers', bank clerks', insurance
      men's,
School teachers', preachers', priests', and
      undertakers'
Eyes sucking in the stimulating light.

Why have they trained, shod, dressed and
      painted
Adorned themselves so?
What liar's lie calls this plain beauty?
Someone with a knowledge of explosive
      chemistry,
Someone who wants to watch the shimmering
      light
Eat up the empty darkness.

What is the lust that paints these eyes?
The barbershop's canon lied,
The booming message that they want us
As we want them sells magazines, sells
      haircuts,
But they are sold, who therefore buy them.
What do the exquisite creatures want,
What is their lust that we may know them?
Eyes watch, eyes pry, the brotherhood ponders,
Betrays a doubt, bewilderment,
What makes them tick?
In the beauty parlor, the sisterhood,
Incants its full-voiced mysteries,
Reads its gnostic gospel tracts,
Catechizes and anoints.

Berobed and sitting in the throne,
The young man watching the mirror
Sees the window, sees the sidewalk,
Seizes opportunity now and again,
The form and face of woman,
The mirrored glance, the eyes.
The spinning pole says naught to her,
Her eyes find meaning nowhere here,
Except in turning heads and eyes,
His eyes, not what they look like, no,
But where they look, their looking.

This is holy writ to her,
The tracing of the eyes of men,
A power they reveal as hers
To pull, to catch, to rule.
Who watches from a throne
Through the accurate mirror?
Who is robed in splendor
Sees and seizes?
He does not ask it -- does she?

The lust of the eyes, the brotherhood's bond,
Has only this one higher echo,
In the schoolgirl's eyes, the woman's eyes
Of the sisterhood, a distillation,
A purer and more awful desire,
The lust to be lusted after,
And thereby to control -- to bind Samson,
No ache of flesh, but spirit,
Acting out Eve's worser curse,
The dull pain unrelieved by birth.

Going to, and coming from,
In the barbershop, male eyes stare,
Each lusting unto itself,
Exacerbating one another, but alone,
Longing to lure and overcome
One who thinks the overcoming hers.
The mirror-windows show double images
Of unfulfilled seeking unfulfillment,
Down the deceiving semaphoric
Signals of sent sight.

And now and again a glance is caught
While down some tunnel of vision
Deep sounds to shallow,
Sounds too deep.
She catches him catching her,
And thinks he wants her
Who wants only his own desire,
Lust and lust for lust,
Conjoin in mantis mating,
Fruitless coupling in which both are consumed.

IV. HOW DO YOU WANT IT?

How do _you_ want it, buddy?

THE FOUR HUMOURS

His temperament is phlegmatic, look how long
His life, his plans, his patience last,

How slow he is (though very strong)
To do his threats and promise past.

He is melancholy, to be sure, so minute
His work; careworn his figure;
His sweat, tears but that humour's fruit,
That tree alone could bear such rigor.

Choleric, dictatorial, he -- angry, intent on
      order.
The history of his reign is clear:
His commandments long, his patience shorter,
Fall heaviest on those he holds most dear.

Sanguine, he is, with such far-flung doings,
And ever extreme in joy and sorrow,
Forgetting the harder things he has said;
Has blood in excess we may borrow.

JIM JONES

The God-damned bastard!
Product of what illicit marriage --
American gullibility
And church's miscarriage --
Brought forth wind, a Satan's son.
His flock of foolish
All empty under the sun.
How could it happen?
How couldn't it.
When the glory departs
Nothing's left but shit.

Brightly covered carcasses
In attitudes of prayer
Nothing can preserve
From the Germ in the air.
Genemata echidna! Son of snakes
In your jungle purple
Drink away your shakes.
Your cup of blessing
Wasn't the worst.
When did you first taste
The cup of the cursed?
Jim Jones, hateful man,
Millstone-necked liar --
Calling mountains down on you
From eternal fire.
Woe to you! Woe to us!
Woe to any one
Who worships any man but
The God-blessed Son!

BETWEEN APRIL FOOLS' AND EASTER

Mae Nagel passed out of this world
The day before Easter,
The day after April Fools',
Between two holidays of the pagan
      calendar,
Two celebrations of the equinox.
Death did not surprise her,
Night suddenly wide as day,
Nor did she miss the resurrection
Swallowing up darkness,

For one took nails in his hands,
An April Fool, promising a fairer May.
Her room is strangely bare,
Her wheelchair folded empty.

MOUSE TRAP

This week we caught the city mouse
And his six country cousins,
Broke up their happy establishment
In the bottom of the china cupboard.
While setting it the other night
The trap went off in my hand,
Drawing a thirty year old memory to the bait:

Mousetraps I played with on the back porch
Spending much pain
Beside sand boxes where carrots lasted all
        winter
Near the side room with the high bed
With the white spread faint with fair odors
Where Grandmother's image lingered
From before she died of cancer.
No, say Mom and Dad, it was we
Who slept there those first years,
But my imagination is sealed in amber.
That back porch with the gray pine floor
Seemed incredibly ancient, museum-like,
The gone-to-dust motes hanging in the still air.
Her I dimly remember in a hospital room
In a bed beside which I tiptoe kissed
An almost impossible reminiscence.

But where did it come from?
What trap, set by whom with what bait
In the back porch of memory,
Has caught this mouse or finger now?

YOU REST

At the funeral mourners breathe oppressive
      silence,
Unnaturally still. Granite gates read "Rest In
      Peace".

Silence, stillness, rest
Imposed on the quick and the long slow.
Oppressive silence, unnatural stillness,
And an incantation against the departed.

Nothing is more foreign, nothing more
      difficult,
Nor more to be feared than to be silent, be still,
      to rest.
We fill our days with loud frantic hurry rather
Than stop. Listen. And find peace.

Like a lamb before the slaughter he was silent,
Says be still and know that I am God, and
Come you weary and heavy-laden --
I will give you rest.

James Howard Trott

NOT THERE

Time is not a segment of eternity, part of a
  long line,
But created transience suspended in wide
  fixity.
Thus it is Frances, our grandmother-sister,
As she approaches permanence where
  mortality ceases,
Occasionally loses track, seeing and talking
  with
Her sisters and mother, long gone, some say.
But who are we to tell her they are not there?
It is we who are not there -- yet.

BOBBY

The tent itself appeared uninhabitable,
Constricted, awry, grotesque.
When he moved in, so he told a friend,
The repairman said it couldn't last.
Seventy-two years it lasted, long enough.

But out of that tent, stretched and
  contorted,
Came the most wonderful signs --
Supernatural unsung songs,
And barely comprehensible glorious
  rejoicings.
None could pass by without marveling
At the contrast of house and householder.

Yet all he had was that slack-sinewed
      space
Mysteriously knit by one tentmaker
Who hems in all he loves,
And for those who love him --
Works all threads together for good.

The tent was a gift to Bobby,
Bobby a gift to us,
That we might learn to long for more
      fitting
Bodies, and dwellings, and home.

ON INATTENTION

Supposed senility and childish inattention
Are not imbecile as they appear.

Even the most blank of nursing home faces
Is a well-kept journal, though often written
In a hand so fine few bother to read.

After a Christmas concert during which she
      sat still
No more than thirty seconds at a time,
My two year old sang tunes and words,
Many perfectly, having heard them but once.

Youth and age put no stock in appearing
      attentive,
Nor dissemble as they listen,
Refusing to make hearing an act.

It is these middle years in which deceit
Is cultivated in this and other things.
We smile nicely as we listen
To words we despise, fearing to show it,
Inwardly full of vituperation, damning
What youth and age know but to ignore.
Carefully we set our eyes, heads, and faces
In postures of fascination, pretended hearing,
While our minds dither, imbecile,
Far away, mulling over some sweet crust,
Senile and childish indeed.

OTHERS LIVES
"The tears of the sower and the songs of the reaper
Shall mingle together in joy bye and bye."
-- OLD HYMN

We live each others lives.
Others our hopes fulfill;
Others live out dreams and dreads
We don't nor ever will.

Some of the brightest visions
And nightmares, dark and long,
Are lived out by some other --
His words to our song.

We grudge sometimes the life he leads,
He lusts for what we've done,
Unless we take our lives as loans --
One sum from one someone.

Then live we this our own for them,
They theirs on our behalf,
And toss up longing for another's lot
As the thresher tosses chaff.

THE PITCHERS

The potter threw them, homely vessels
Meant for water or for wine
Of mud mixed, clay and water,
Well-fired, but not so fine
The women didn't give them gladly
For the task conceived so madly:
Gideon and his God-mad sappers,
His poor tithe-troop of water lappers --
No need of pitchers in their uncivilized
      tents anyway.

They were carried growing hot
Into the camp of the undefeated.
All had something hidden in them
Which their brittle bodies heated.
All their earthly use was ended
As the breaking trumpets blended,
Pitchers shivered into shards
Overcame the night-eyed guards.
Light poured out of broken jars, made of
      shabby clay.

SISYPHUS

The stone of Sisyphus gathered no moss.
For the king of Corinth life was a loss --
No time for games or pretty ladies
Working on a hill in Hades.

It's said that Hell's a fearsome pit,
Rumored but few have climbed from it.
Good Sisyphus, then should make no bones
About his task of rolling stones.

If he could reach his hell-hill's top
He'd find that was no place to stop
And he'd go on to harder phases,
Struggling up the walls of Blazes.

And if he did get out in time,
There'd be some Everest left to climb.
Yet surely his task has all the worth
Of upwardly mobile man's on earth.

THE PRESSURE-TREATED CROSS

Epiphany has filled the empty stonework
        houses
Up with old rejoicing --
New rejoicings, too, and
New ways of remembering,
Looking forward to what was
And, oh, what shall be.
Before the edifice of rock

(How we love the thought
Of buildings laid on cornerstones)
They raised a new cross this Eastertide,
Which I just saw
Now that it's empty:
Two machine-milled
Beams of recently popularized
Pressure-treated lumber,
Guaranteed not to rot
Even when stuck away
In the damp and dark,
Laid down or buried in
Soil of corrupting earth.
The pale green wood,
Saturated with salts
Which drive out all the things
Wood is heir to,
Looked like a mockery at first,
Before the gray-stone piety,
Yet it wasn't meant nor can it be.
Even the ugliest of man's works
(Crosses ugly in all places)
Will point the four ways
Where God is found:
Pressure-treated, salt-soaked,
Dry unto thirsting,
On the green wood of preservation.

ROAD KILL

In the dusky dim of daunted day
Before obliterating snow,

The panting doe crossed from woods to
     field,
Crossed a narrow road
Where shriek of horn and rubber tires
Faded with impact of fender and life.
The dusk dimmer, the day more daunted,
I came along the road of execution,
Saw the blur of white and tan
Like a mystical presence along my path --
Something sacrificed, yet wholesome,
Brought down and offered to me, waiting --
For me to load it on my vehicle,
To hurry home, no longer weary,
Full of news and anticipation
Of good meat, freely taken,
Clearly a provision,
Like the scouring snow
Which fell that evening,
Making the whole earth white.

KNOWING

By arcane wisdom known to me --
My gnosis -- I call that illusory
Which I can see or touch or smell --
Heaven is Nothing; this is hell.

By ratio and rationale
My science proves and proves it well
That there is naught but what we see,
Nothing but matter (and energy).

Gnostic knowing and science's sense --
No liege; "knowledge," pounds without pence,
Ignorance decked in the king's new clothes,
Manger dogs growling at -- Who Knows.

MARCH POEM

The March wind loves to touch my face.
To caress me to a blush beneath the stoking
     sun,
And there is music in the trees,
Top-tossing threnodies and steady sighs
Of anguish and ennui.
Yes, there is poetry in the air --
Poetry so thick you can cut it with a pen.
It is March and I am a March poet.
I will take a vow to write for March alone,
To fast from ink and paper all the year
But this brief noon
In which life returns with fury;
Hot life rages against cold death
And overthrowing briefly, then driven back --
Amidst bursting signals of beleaguered armies
-- In the white explosions of clouds -- rushing --
I am rushing. Together
March and I are rushing toward our life,
Our home.

NO RETURN

Grandfather, a Chicago boy, hunted bottles

At the money-poor, time-rich turn of the
  century,
Stood outside forbidden swinging doors
Waving each back and forth
In sight of unseen liquor sellers
Until, marking him, one emerged to pay
A penny for the booty.
Some things change so slowly
We hunted bottles at mid-century,
Children of world wars, grandchildren
Of untold interim breakthroughs,
Found soda glass "pop" bottles in the park
Along the running river further west.
In cool groceries, less forbidding,
Phlegmatic clerks redeemed ours for three
  cents.
A decade later Pacific bottle-hunters crossed
  back
The high divides and dug their ways
From west to east without regard
For dumps and heaps, ghost towns, neglected
  farms,
Salvaging old penny glass to sell for stakes
Which would have made barkeepers stare,
Rush wildly out the tavern doors
To hunt for bottles then, themselves.
Now grandfather is gone and swinging doors;
Bottles read no return.

DEFEAT

West is true brother to the South,

Though younger.
Deep south cannot forget defeat,
A haunting ghost, gone glory.
The North, as South calls it
(Back-east says West)
Lives on in myths of its own making:
Victory out of rebellion
Against King and God;
Victory, again, against depraved rebels.
South fought the king, too,
But turned back in sackcloth
Before the latter prophet, defeat.
The West (short of Saint Andrew's fault)
Knows defeat, as well,
Nor needs look back to be reminded.
Wide prairie and plateau,
Stone-staring mountain proclaim
Man lingers here by sufferance,
Nor ever had glory to speak of.
Defeat digs deep into the land,
Delves depth of mind and soul.

THE WILD ROSES AND THESE

Where roses grew down the coulee cleft
We smelled them in summer, their blossoms
        we left.
We left them for beetles, for bees, for all,
We left them for rosehips to pick in the fall.
Here redder roses, but far fewer bloom.
We grow them to look at, to smell their
        perfume.

We pick them as soon as the bright petals fade:
For love of their beauty, their future we trade
For the hope of other buds, precious each one --
No hips redden here when summer is done.
Rosehips, they tell us, are vitamin rich;
Perhaps it's a scurvy trick blossoms to snitch,
But we must pick these, buds to renew,
-- As other lives blossom where rosehips grew.

ELEGY FOR DALE NOTTINGHAM

Death rushes upon the shore
And crashes down, forcing all before it,
Then rushing back it pulls, does not release,
But draws all with it; none resists.

The rock of ages stand a time
As chips fly white from ocean mountains:
Granites go, bit by bit, and in the night
Nothing lasts but a moment -- all opposing
       surrenders.

The boulder breaks, the pine is uprooted,
The fawn and the stag are caught and sink
       and drown,
But the seal swims, outswims the surf,
Surrenders to the wave and rides the deep
       unconquered.

The seal, eternal, is born on the rocks
Among his kind, his mate, and his calf.

When he is gone into the never-ceasing swell
      and crash
Beneath the pounding death he rides the sea,
And rides it home.

INNOCENT QUERY

And what does a rabbit say? my son asked,
Which innocent query sent my mind
Leaping back across the gaps and thickets
To a fawn, by way of
"They don't say anything,
Except when they are young or afraid.
Then they cry like babies."

When his mother and I were in Montana
With Adriel, his sister, in arms,
We made our way under barbed wire
Up from my uncle's cabin in the high woods
Through thick scrub growth.
There we came upon the creature.

We'd gotten between him and his mother
Or frightened her so badly
She abandoned him in flight.
But how we frightened him --
For with unearthliest whinnying moans
He ran back and forth before us.

Adriel, in fear or sympathy, cried too.
Somewhere a hidden hart started.

But grown deer, like grown rabbits,
Are said to be mute.

TRYGVE BIRKELAND

The missionary novels a classmate brought
Across the Samaria of sixth grade,
The choruses of Marconi angels,
The prayers of aunts and cousins
Might never have fetched me
Were it not for the tall phantom
Of Trygve Birkeland pursuing
Through the Methodist halls of memory
With Washington Irving relentlessness.
I encounter him still,
Memory merging into mythos,
At the inner of the double doors
Leading to the antique sanctuary
From which in full-flung childish flurry
I ran fleeing like an infidel.
The door caught his high Norse forehead,
A blow that brought the blood welling
From above his eye into my vision,
Whereupon I fled back in wrath-wraithed fear.
Skirting thereafter about dim halls
And cross-close chambers,
(In one of which a long rope hung
Linked to venerable heaven,
Rumored to be too cracked to speak)
I awaited the judgment I knew I deserved.
But when I encountered Trygve at last,
That day, and down the weeks and years,

There never fell one well-earned "crucify!"
Upon my shriveling curse-tuned ears,
Or my law-abiding parents', no --
Only hoarse kindness, the patient humour
Of broken-bodied, long-suffering grace,
Bloody-headed, haunting forgiveness.

PRETEND NOT ACROSS THE GAPS

Pretend not across the gaps.
The filling of time and space
Have always been sad industries.

Transportation does not bridge continents,
But transforms land, rivers, seas
Into cinematic frauds.

No late-breaking news is current,
Nor do period pieces or science fiction
Conjoin a now and a then.

Pretend not across the gaps.

Rests and infinitesimal spaces
Between notes make music
As fully as chords and tones,
Themselves internally syncopated
With troughs and crests.

Collapsing bridges and skywalks
Great manmade catastrophes
Fell because babbling builders

Thought to quickly fill
Broad ethers with their flimsy plans.

Such things bear witness
To the function of hiatus.

Most terrible is our slick inclination
To dump loose earthfill words
And crumbling thoughts into the chasms
Separating ourselves and others
Or lying vast between God and man.

Pretend not across the gaps.

CICADA CYCLE

I. TO AN HOMOPTERAN

You've sirened me with your sun stark
      note,
Softened my tightening shell for a split,
Lured me out of my beaten earth track,
To look through compound eyes and see;
Stop my nymphal crawl; become somewhat
Homo sapiens flying on your wings,
Perplexed by the wisdom folded there and
      elsewhere.
But I'm intent on sucking sap from tree
      roots
Until I'm mature enough for branches.
I drink my earth-clogged eyes full of you,
Feel some strange quickening.

II. CICADA NYMPH

I have seen the willow-the-wisp
Whose ghosts hang among bushes and trees,
Whose haunting husks crackle underfoot
In summer woods and on shaded lawns.
Keeping an eye peeled for fellow travelers,
I found one once near a lake in Japan;
Two, now, in two summers, closer to home.
These insignificant, slow-crawling creatures,
 Are awkward, passive, defenseless, though
                clawed,
Burnt-brown with a faint hint of green
In those brief buds which might be wings.
The clay sticking to their smooth-shelled
                backs
Bespeaks a subterranean origin.
All three ignored me, my moon-loomed face,
My molesting hands,
They had some sense of destiny
Which compelled them toward their places
                and times
With no regard for me.
The Japanese nymph was a nocturnal monk,
Emerged at late evening for his mystical
                ritual.
Second met was a retarded creature,
Whose mid-morning metamorphosis
                mesmerized me.
Now a third, early morning riser
Reaffirms findings, the infinite in the
                infinitesimal.

These strange creatures like mobile jewels
With unmechanical intricacies,
Were radiant, dark in fluid colors
With a flowing life that still courts awe
And splits this wonder out of me.

III. ON THE EMERGENCE OF A CICADA

This locust lost his tabled time
Somewhere in seventeen years,
Or so I must suppose,
Since insect experts thus direct:
All such emerge in darkness.
This cicada, confused, traumatized,
Or otherwise aberrant,
Came from the ground one July morning,
A nymph yet, and kept on --
Kept on in the cycle which,
Experts agree, goes back many eons.
He climbed the trunk of a nearby tree,
Perhaps the one upon roots of which
He had subsisted decade and seven,
And made his way along the trunk
Despite forelegs built for digging.
There in the morning sun he split,
Tore ancient skin right down the back,
Emerged a pale and different thing.
Slowly his nubs of wings were filled
Until they stretched to twice his length.
There, hanging from ruins of his older self,
He became firm and hard, a new creature,
Which flew away.

IV. A PARTURITION

Not satisfied with the high arc,
The graceful curve of her back,
The nymph set her feet and strained
In strangest labor.
The birth compulsion sprung
From no womb but her being.
No child squeezed from her protected belly
Into the murderous world.
No, her very shoulders parted,
Spreading wide her back
As she struggled to bear herself over.
The sleek dark beauty of her mysterious body
Was ruined in the hideous effort,
To be left a crackling shell.
The split-coat humpback creature
Strained through her disfigurement
Toward the birth of her new self.

V. PROGRESS BY CRAWLING

Your progress on the surface
Is so painful especially in light
Of all the preparation gone before,
Unrealized potential,
But laboring like a steadfast workman
Through the years of your sojourn,
Not despairing over tediousness or tears,
Keeping patiently to the secrets of your guild,
Not knowing yourself your own best
        workmanship.

VI. THE CICADA KILLER

I thought the code the cicada sent
The telegram tattling through the trees,
Was fully enough to sustain my attention,
Was subtle enough to while the day,
Without your fierce prospect.
But now you've grasped me in your six legs
Impaled me over and over until
You've pickled my frantic imagination
With your wise venom,
Dragged me down into your halls of soil
And laid the hatching eggs, your young,
Which even now begin to feed and grow
On my living thoughts.

VII. PROGENY

Up from the deepest, dirt-bound roots
The locust came. Now from the height
As luggage steep trajectory drops.
The wasp carried him home to her hole,
Tunnel beneath, again, the ground,
From which he had escaped.
On the tree the wasp her prey
Pierced, subdued and carried captive,
Up the trunk to top of conquered kingdom,
From which to launch her victory flight.
The tree was through
With the buzz, the weight
Of the tiny sipping, little-sapping thing,
Except for the minute spheres, the eggs
His mate lays in the scars of twigs,

Soon to hatch into antlike nymphs,
Which tumbling down over earth around
Will tunnel down and begin again.
And in the cicada-killer's rooms,
His enemy's children eat the living cicada.

HOLDING HANDLED HANDS

The father's hand is the child's favorite toy,
New digits articulating old.
Tender tentative, barely knitted
Exert full strength to hold the stained,
The long rough, and strange restrained.
Small eyes, light-touched,
Intently map each branching line,
Guide small surveyors with measured chains
Over each furrow, callous, scar,
Across canyons, ridges of tissued time.
Untaught infant sensibility
Fingers wounds in fascination:
Wondering fingertips and nails
Trace mysterious records
Of building, skill, accident, and pain.
Fingers hold hands held fingers, many,
Digits stretch toward time unblemished
When a child hallowed hands, his own,
Star-blotting fingers joined tiny joints.
Held, himself, fascinated,
A father folds his hands to hold
The everlasting holding him.

WASPS IN AUTUMN

In the fall the Hymenoptera,
Membrane-winged named, ordered insects,
Are the first to whiff winter.
As sister bees labor at larders
And brother ants fill tunneled bins,
Wasps, cruel cousins, fear their ends
From first hint of cold to come.
They change their ways: becoming fiercer,
Sharp-stinging raiders, offensive scouts,
Patrolling lawns and eaves of houses.
It seems to us they have gone mad:
Hovering, threatening, diving down,
And ranging around us at our lunches,
But they have nothing stored to save
Themselves from frosty wind and snow.
Perhaps they are becoming sane --
For this lash out with angry logic:
Futile existentialists
Hoping to leave some mark, some memory,
If only pang of remembered pain,
To signify their desperate passage
Before meeting some bleak end.

ON PRESERVING PROMISES

The promises of God wear thin in time:
Manna no longer stinks, lilies no longer mime
In the city of the world.
There are rivers, there are trees,

There are birds of the air, but few consider
    these.
The fields are gone, flocks and cattle unheard-
    of.
The priesthood has changed, tidied temples,
    acts of love.
No blood or smoke fills porticos with doubt,
The money-changing is within, no saver is cast
    out.
The meat is in the deep-freeze, securities may
    be bought:
Unseen, they are believed in; assured, they are
    sought.
No one hopes for a land: plowing, sowing,
    gleaning,
Sojourners, harvest, tares . . . all have lost their
    meaning.
We have subdued all things, built towers,
    barns, ships.
God's promises wear thin enough to slide
    between our lips.

DARK SHADOW

A dark shadow, small and mean
Towers the years beyond each child
In the shadowbox of imagination,
Fills waking dreams with vague dreads.
Yet the eye, or the mind's eye,
Sees time, neither lame nor halt,
Run fears backward
As childish shadows grow and yet

Are swallowed by the foraging light.
Radiant, bright and taller than Babel,
The unseeable cross pulls shadows in --
See the living child of God
Light from each child the shades of sin.

IMITATION

Who flatters, batters. Have a care how he
    pretends --
Imitation is the sincerest form of revenge.

SPRING LOVERS

Once upon an ancient time
Lovers in spring made me sigh,
But now the chances they're husband
    and wife --
To somebody else is too high.

ORACULAR DYSFUNCTIONS

Speaking without unctions,
Cowardly compunctions,
Alimentary rambunctions,
Adverbs (and) conjunctions.

JOINING A CHURCH
(from a comment by John Julien)

Be cautious in joining for heaven's sake --
This is no club, it is a jail-break.

FOREBODING

These things have haunted me all my days,
A poem, a dream, a kinsman's ways;
Of a book, the title; another of a song --
All have assured me I would go wrong.

I DON'T KNOW WHY

Satan Fell.   So did I.
God caught me -- I don't know why.

WET SLEEPING BAGS

The children could not resist –
Their active part was but the refrain.

Their baggy bedding was doubly damped,
By onomatopoeia with the rain.

EVERY MAN

Every man has studied for the cold killer's
        place,
Every woman has achieved belle-*dame-sans-*

merci's face.
Insouciance has won the day, iniquity the
      night.
All locked in rigid masks to frighten off fright.

EPITAPH

He died I fear as did his nation
From some excess of moderation.

REMEMBERED PRAYER

Oh Lord,
Remember the dry bones
Which fleshed and re-membered
Remembered you.

THE PRESBYTERIAN

His head knew the heart of God,
Better than his heart God's head.
Since God's heart and head are one,
He half-understood what he said.

WOMAN ENOUGH

If the metaphor is good enough,
Points of contact and divergence
Serendipitous to the finest feeling of a good gut,

It will have a universality
Which allows for various application.
The sun has presumably been sun since before
    the moon,
But peoples in all places have called it god or
    lover.
God or lover or truth or life or hope or rebirth...
    If the metaphor is good enough.
If a man is man enough or a woman woman
    enough,
They are very much like each other and may
Perhaps be types or tropes for various things,
Or for each other -- be more than
Metaphors for someone beyond the sun.

IDOL-MAKING MACHINE
"Our hearts are idol-making machines"
--John Calvin

Hearts churn out their little gods.
Built for better, gone awry.
Heads make reasons, flesh sensations,
Hearts stamp idols, tool and die.

Idols are not evil stuff --
Wood for carving, wood for burning,
Gold for molding, gilding, shining.
Such were good were it enough.

But hearts are god-assembly lines,
Turning good to God-blot bad.
Take each gift and soon deform it,

Driving all creation mad.

Hearts are idol-minting presses,
Stamping out their worthless tin,
While our minds and voices hawk them,
Barkers 'midst the factory din.

If God does not foreclose, dismantle,
Forge anew, and scourge each clean,
All are bound to mindless pounding,
Heartless idol-mints, machines.

A SICKLY LEAF

The sickly yellow leaf, obscene and gaunt,
Against the dark wet trunk which grew it,
Dropped and sailed in light wide spirals,
Among the others holding their moment.

It soars, apparently free and graceful,
Freer it seems than they.
Perhaps more than living makes them green -

-

Green also with envy.

TO AN ARACHNID

I suppose we are all daughters of dyers,
        Arachne,
And all great weavers against the gods,
Rescued from heavenly revenge only by

Olympian pity.

Why do you cling then, so determined to your
 web?
Why I, to my little nets and railings?

To yourself, and of course your flies,
You are of great significance, crafting now
Your own embraces, no longer mindful of the
 gods'.

And when you fall from shock or fear
Down upon the solid rock, rooted in the heart
 of things,
You are so uncomfortable, and so quick to
 scramble
Back up a familiar filament to your own warp
 and woof.

What if this being confronting you, driving you
 out,
Is greater than Athena -- not jealous at all, but
 purer,
And means better things for you than sucking
 at flies,
Than clinging, near-sighted to your own poor
 web?

BRAKE FOR ANIMALS

If nature had been red in tooth and claw at first

-

No one vegetarian -- perhaps we'd not be
      cursed.
If God had made the larder less scant --
Allowed every animal as well as every plant...
But it was not so. Those early vegetarians
Were partial to fruit, steaks were post-
      lapsarian.
Vegetable clothes, too, were hastily discarded
The day of their invention -- the God hard-
      hearted
Enough to slaughter beasts clothed sinners in
      skins,
As they returned the compliment, getting
      sinners in sins.
Cain the first Romantic, with worship unsuited
To the new environment, offered what he'd
      fruited,
While Abel offered bloody meat -- of some new
      worth --
And Abel's blood was heard crying from earth.
When God could no longer stand the din-
      stench of men,
He set Noah aside to begin again,
He made a zoo (no greenhouse on the ark)
That deaths might go on in the post-flood park.
Animals and men alike perished in the flood,
World full of water mixed with world full of
      blood.
Man, by God's word, then became omnivorous,
Eater of all things, vegetarian carnivorous.
Noah offered sacrifice, no Cain-like salad,
But every clean beast and bird, which God
      found valid.

Among the strange changes in the post-flood
       features
God made covenant with all the creatures.
In ritual uncivilized, before anti-vivisection,
Abraham made bloody pledge, at God's
       direction,
And cut up heifer, goat, ram, pigeon, dove.
That night God promised Abraham his love.
Deeds lead to divers deeds -- such things
       begun,
Abraham went up a hill to offer up his son.
God provided blood, another became damned,
The substitute for Isaac, a thorn-horn-hung
       ram.
Esau had a taste for game, his father did, too.
Jacob dual-fooled them with kid and bean
       stew.
Birthright-blessed Jacob blanched at blood of
       goat
-- Joseph sold, his brothers saved the blood-
       soaked coat.
Delivered by that will which works ill things
       well,
Israel brought livestock with baaing and bell.
High Egypt loathed shepherds then (tidy to a T)
Fastidiousness Pharaoh, Moses' dupe, thus set
       free
Israel, blood being Egypt's abomination, after
Creature plagues, darkness and blood swept
       the nation.
The angel of death came and struck Egypt's
       core,
While other firstborn flourished, behind

bloody doors.
Full of wonder and joy through another flood's
drowning,
To receive rules of blood they went, amidst
earth's groaning,
A bloodless calf was praised while Moses met
God.
It could not make atonement, therefore cost
much blood.
Many years and hard hearts passed in desert
sorrows,
But sacrifice continued -- blood of beasts
borrowed.
Entering at last with abundant sheep and cattle,
Joshua subdued the land in pitched bloody
battle.
But the pagan ways of pagan-kind, not forgot
forty years,
False gods and altars brought on more blood
and tears,
Down to subtle Saul whose great piety boded
Ill for his line when he kept flocks devoted.
David planned, Solomon built for God-
ordained slaughter --
Blood of animals poured out like rivers of
water.
Long rivers of blood went unceasing to pay
For rivers of sin with one small hope, a day
Sacrifice sufficient would save -- a mysterious
king,
Who would offer a pure lamb, the last offering,
A servant despised, whose blood for all strays,
Lamb's for sheep-like men, would suffice

always.
Last prophet, John, dressed in skins of camels,
Said "Behold God's lamb," let us brake for
    animals.
Speaking better things than blood of goats and
    bulls,
His dripped from a cross to wash stained souls.
The throat of God, sin-parched, no more thirsts
    for blood,
Neither man's blood or animals -- it is finished
    -- for good.

A BULLET PROOF TRAIN

The will of God is a bullet-proof train;
A gain without loss, a loss without gain;
A jeweler's window, a thief in the night;
A blow in the dark, warm arms of light.

No traveler goes by safer mean;
No fare cheaper, no ticket steeper.
No hoard so bright, no surprise as obscene;
No harder knock, no gentler shock.

The will of God hurtles through to its end
At negligible cost, every mite you spend;
Every gem cut, every safe rifled;
A complete knockout, all pain stifled.

The darts bounce off, the express arrives;
Every labourer paid, each wageless strives;
The jewel thief breaks the shop window in;

Night blotted out God; Jesus kissed away sin.

SHOPLIFTING

The prices rise, in large part, they say
Because every dog must have his day,
Every kleptomaniac, every quick slick shifter
Must get his free and be shop-lifter.

Some of us, righteous, more thoroughly
      proper
Call ourselves, not lifter, but second-hand
      shopper.
We return for fruit we were not weighed for
Picking up old sins Christ bought and paid
      for.

A CHARM

Dither, dither, dithyramb,
Down beside the river ran
The moonbeams, how they thither swam
Until the night grew wither wan.

Sawnie, sawnie, sonneteer,
In the woods a-waxing queer
As the mountains and the deer
Rose and trembled all in fear.

Bally, bally, ballad-tale

On the waves and under sail
O'er the moor and in the dale
The moon sunk low as though to fail.

Maidy, maidy, maiden's prayer,
Whispered 'cross the cold night air
Flying sweet where no songs fare
With truer words than poets dare.

SNAKES AND TREES

Some ambitious psychologist holds
The roots of mankind's diseases
Are found in the men of the ancient dark
        glens
Who fought with the snakes from the treeses.

Now the snakes of those times, those tropical
        climes
Were none of them tiny or docile.
They were horrid and huge -- the only refuge
From their jaws were those trees gone to
        fossil.

The reptilian hoard, with its manners
        untoward
Likewise is the most part extinct,
One wonders why theorists hold theories the
        dearest
Which must be gymnastically thinked.

NOT CONTENT WITH MERE. . .

Not content with mere morning
He scalded the dew
With dropped down sun-pink
And lit the world before it had begun.

Not content with mere evening
He wreathed the brow
Of the moon in mist
And comforted the world when it was dark.

Not content with mere climates
He ordered the differences
Of summer, spring, winter, fall
And varied their coming beyond prediction.

Not content with mere justice
He sent his son
With full forgiveness --
So he might be content with mere me.

SINGING ON THEIR KNEES

The hilarious chorus which bewildered
    summer's night
Has sung the house down, the last leaves alight
Along the aisles and all outdoors astrew
With brown-gold debris awaits winter's cue.

But though they have traveled, danced, drunk
    and mated,

Scattered chorus voices chant on. Unsated,
They no longer call each to each. Each his own
Last notes of longing sings thinly, alone.

Katy-did, Katy-didn't, Katy is no more.
Cicadas, loud fanatics, dinned death in the
      door.
But chirping crickets linger and their cousins in
      the trees,
These aging chorus creatures are singing on
      their knees.

It is a chorus yet -- no riot, now -- ethereal.
Feebly in the hedgerows like mourners at a
      burial,
Or from the willow weeping yellow leaf tears,
The tree crickets' harps ring weak though clear.

Some melody haunts them -- one they should
      forget;
Frost fingers trace their doom, about them
      weave a net.
Why don't they cease, desist: go silent to their
      end . . .
Unless a cricket is a song -- what might that
      portend?

INSTANT AND ETERNAL

Instant and eternal are the acts of God,
Without hiatus, without end.
Finished and unending

Are his breaths and his hammer-blows.
There is no second chance with him,
There is no last chance with him:
His judgment is over -- and it will never come
-- For those who have entered
Into his instant and eternal grace.

EMPTY

We reconsider like returning dogs:
'Waste not want not' -- a goodly theme.
Morsels once tasty might prove so again,
Prove exceptions this recent regurgitation.

My stoic stomach suffers long
Before giving in to humiliation --
Promised relief is not prize enough
To lure me down to abandonment.

Not dog, not mind-over-master-man knows
How good it is to stay emptied,
Bow at last and play the fool:
Release the fierce restraints of heart
Pour out hideous and leave it in peace --
As far as purged west from dog-gone east.

PORT IN STORM

Thoughts surge and flow around my head,
Words row like little boats
Seeking a port, a place to land,

Enduring form, a reach, a strand.

Drifting over all comes time's salt,
Which halts metre while slim rhyme's
Compass spins in age's fog
Where bouys warn at odds with the log.

Like the ancient mariner's phantom sea
My mind is pickled in obscurity,
And stands still under doldrum's arm.
Or contrary gales of desire engage
To flap and tear each sail-sheet's page.
But, ahoy! Most come to port in storm.

CRUSTY BREAD AND INSUFFICIENT WINE

A poor meal as meals go, although there's none
    to blame,
No one especially -- no host, of course.
The bread to the best of my perception
Was a large roll of Italian family,
Downright tough, so that Tim in the first row,
Had to work hard to extricate his piece.
The wine was not wine, nor ever is.
(I often wish. . . because of the difference
Between poetry and false advertising,
Metaphor and balderdash,
Between faith and politics.)
And we ran out of that sweet juice
Three rows from the back.
Tom dashed out and quickly got a few
    tumblers more,

Though that didn't cover it, either,
But by the book the elders marched back
Up the aisles, as though we'd done all we
      ought,
And sat down to share, with the back two
      rows,
A cup-less communion.
But gracious John -- the body has no crust --
Gently apologized and asked couples to share.
Soon a brother and sister brought up
Four more crystal plastic thimblefulls
Of wine, indeed, humility, love,
And we ate and drank to the table of heaven --
Lord's supper, communion, and eucharist.

IF I WERE TO DESIGN THE UNIVERSE

    Every Jekyl would have his Hyde,
    Every Laurel his Hardy,
    That's how I would plan the list
    If I had a party.

    I would have teetotalers
    To consume the soda,
    And a few social drinkers
    To imbibe the booze quota.

    I would have no wall-flowers,
    Or have them by twos,
    With a few matchmakers
    To compel them to choose.

I would have everyone jolly,
No one would be sad,
Everyone would dance,
None prove a cad.

There would be no weak Adam,
No ambitious Eve,
No forbidden tree,
With a snake up its sleeve.

There would be no
Jewish-Gentile division
No Barnabus and Paul
To fight about mission,

No thorns in the flesh,
No belly-achin' --
Nor would I ever die
To save anybody's bacon.

BY ASSEMBLAGES OF THINGS

By assemblages of things, I have found,
I can win praise, a moment's renown.

I labor mothlike to grow wings --
In this chrysalis -- out of things.

Seeking riches: a name of gold, no more,
I have emptied out my hourglass' store.

Seeking to win what I've thus far but leased,

I would sell everything, 'til sellings cease.

Toward what end, these labors and objects --
    what goal?
What sort of assemblage can at last hide my
    soul?

TO A POET

Show the crystals each in its matrix,
Polish not the ancient coin
Seldom in glib explication
Do truth and glory conjoin.

BROKER

For a percentage of what changes hands
The broker is patient with all demands
Of both parties in their chosen transaction
Favoring each and neither faction.

He shows the houses, he buys the stock,
Tailors the policy, absorbs some shock
Of discontent, of diverse expectations,
Makes all he makes in dual relations

Of buyer to seller, grower to miller,
Concern to investor, banker to tiller,
Unique was one who emptied his coffer
Taking the worst either party could offer.

PRAYER UPON A FLOODED BASEMENT

You who set the firmament
Have mercy upon us
Limited the seas extent
Have mercy upon us
Whose flood within a shepherd's heart
Have mercy upon us
Forced Egypt, Israel, sea apart
Have mercy upon us
Who showered good on sinners stark
Have mercy upon us
Even in judgment filling the ark
Have mercy upon us
Who still sends rain upon unjust
Have mercy upon us
Are living water to those who trust
Have mercy upon us.
Prepare me for thy heavenly city
And rescue from drowning in self-pity.
Thy mercy endures forever.
   Amen.

WILD STRAWBERRIES

The bumbling bee and I
Kick a yellow mist from the cloverhead
    beacons,
Neither of us Romantics.
In this after-moon morning in June
He collects a mixture of pollen and nectar

A rather odd mass he carries away
To store in his underground nest and larder
For his unspectacular maggoty progeny.
While I search the dew for strawberries --
Straw'b'ries, my father calls them--
Wild originals, none larger than an acorn,
Most smaller than a pea --
But they are sweet and lead my feet out of
      urban frenzy
Into a pretext of wilderness purpose.
Of course there is no purpose in that sense --
The strawberries are already here,
With no respect due me.
I merely find and pick them,
Gather the small red fragments in a plastic
      basket
Gather them back to my camp-nest.
Both the bee and I bumble
More than is strictly necessary.

THE TONGUE HINGES AT THE HEART -
TWO POEMS

I. HIDDEN THINGS OF THE HEART

The tongue is the doorway to the heart,
The threshold of the soul,
No commerce passes in or out
Unless tongue takes toll.

Words well from dark corners,
Lusts creep from rooms unknown:

The tongue spills rank venom,
Drips desire fresh as foam.

No lock, no curb, no surgery
Can stop its slam or creak
Unless deep down at its root in the heart
It is taught to taste and speak.

II. STOLEN BREAD TASTES SWEET

Stolen bread tastes sweet
Until the day one learns
Omniscience is not discreet,
Responds as it discerns.
Stolen bread tastes sweet
To a tongue that would be slaked --
In longing perpetually poised
No morsel to forsake.

Stolen bread tastes sweet
Except to the alien nation
Groaning long, in longing grown,
Tongues tuned to anticipation.

WHEN DAD GOT SICK AND THE CITY

When Dad got sick and the city
We all rushed in full of boisterous fear and
        joviality
Making horrible gaffes,
And began to assess like junior detectives.
We pushed the healers for all we were worth

To do their job and get to healing.
(Where grief broke in we were embarrassed,
Looking the other way or sheepishly
    apologizing,
Mumbling jokes and the word catharsis.)

When Dad got sick and the city
We brought in our favorite books,
Handing them to him with sacrificial
    sanctimony,
And a gnawing feeling of worthlessness
Which was confirmed for each
By sight of those piled on his table already.

When Dad got sick and the city,
We turned at last like chicks and hens
Those scattered before the hawk --
We wept for Dad and the city.
Knowing we've slept: grieve for that as well.
We are learning to be men of sorrow
Acquainted with grief --
And now to watch and pray.

I WANT NO TASTES OF HEAVEN

I want no tastes of heaven like this,
No more than tastes of hell;
It seems to me more often than not
A hill is next a dell.

The ups and downs make life hard,
So pardon if I demur

When offered ecstatic experience,
No matter how high or pure.

I keep my good in the icebox
To eat as sauce for the bad,
Please, Lord, send no more unspeakable
        joys
Like the sorrow-bound ones we've had!

But he answers, no other kingdom is
Except of darkness or light,
Every in-between is dawn or dusk,
Leading to day or to night.

My joys and my sorrows are yours as mine,
I have no others to give,
You must open your heart to receive both
I offer no filter or sieve,

No means of your own to choose which you
        will --
Your good in the icebox will rot,
But I promise you this the high joys remain
When the deepest sorrow's forgot.

NO TOMORROW

Abraham and the thief on the cross,
Two men with no tomorrow,
Stood at a loss (no gain in sorrow)
Except for the words of God
(Promising more than the luck of a toss?)

One bound for a land,
One bound under sod.
With no tomorrow, better men are unmanned.
These two somehow were able to stand.

THE PROOF

"A sign, a sign," they called for, not
    inhumanly
Looking for something concrete to prove
    "Divine".

Few men thought to wonder, to inquire to
    seek
Evidence empirically establishing "human,"

So well planned, so consummately carried out
The scheme that the whole world was
    compelled

To accept he was a man, once a boy, once
    baby,
Rather than some demi-god or angel or adept:

The persona so much a person that they cried
"A sign," and got none but that of Jonah,

Hard to hear, supposed by most mere rhetoric;
The connection between sin and resurrection
    unclear;

The faith of sometimes bumbling Old

Abraham
By careful niceties and calculations replaced:

The danger, therefore -- although clearly
     signed, "ye shall find
The babe wrapped in swaddling clothes, lying
     in a manger,"

Angel song -- was discounted for theological
     shibboleths
Which, meant to prove the son of man a liar,
     proved wrong.

'TIL DEATH DO US PART

To have and to hold gets the best press, the
     headlines
And the neon lighting in the hurly burly, the
     burlesque
That passes for life, love, marriage.

Our having and holding is often as close to
     union
As Velcro patchwork is a seamless garment.
But we have vowed, you and I, and others, too,
     we both believe,
To have and to hold for better and for worse
'Til death do us part.

That vow, perhaps, was more important for
     ages gone by --
Also for anachronistic us; because otherwise,

They, we, would incline to the opposite heresy
Which makes marriage eternal, against the
      Lord's explicit
Limitation that they neither marry or mate in
      heaven.

Let us then renew this vow of faith.
Having given all and everything to each
Upon this earth and through these days;
We will let all go into larger love,
Into mightier marriage and the lamb's supper
And indeed part at death --
Insofar as need be, at least for that little,
That flicker of time before all joining
Will be one and forever.

ECONOMIZING

If you do not strip the udder
Of your best cow, she'll go dry.
If you focus the job on saving material,
You're bound to lose money on labor.
The efficiency of the kingdom of God
Often turns on empty days and minds --
Hearts unproductive on an earthly scale --
Laying up heavenly treasure.

IN MEMORY OF ISABEL JOHNS

Isabel Johns sat in her chair,
Her sightless eyes watching wheels in the

air,
In a distant corner of a noisome hall,
Waiting for someone to come and call.

Isabel Johns lifted her face
Every time footsteps entered that place:
Listened for words, strained for a greeting,
Like a patient chairman before a meeting.

Isabel Johns sat in her room,
Her dusky face dispelling gloom.
When the angel said, "Come now, cross the
    abyss,"
She lifted her face, said "Give me a kiss."

A CHILD'S DEATH
"Let the little children come to me..."

But Lord -- this haste!
These little ones that rush,
Lord -- the long years' waste!
Their guardian angels, Lord,
Are they so soon weary
That you must take their charges
Lives, barely begun in theory?
Jesus, we're not ready yet:
Had time barely enough to beget,
Grow to love, wonder what they'd be.
It cuts deep -- heart-deep. Lord, do you see?
Say something, shed some light
Into this sorrow, our souls' dark night.
In this great loss what are we taught?

And he answers only "Forbid them not. . ."

Then, Lord, tear-blind, we let go,
In starkest faith, bare belief you know
What you're doing, taking back what you've
        given. . .

"Of such", he says, "are the kingdom of
        heaven."

IAMB

I AM, his meter the penteteuch,
Spoke poems to confound the race,
Asked not only comprehension but response
Iam ("now" in Roman and every place).

Ian the Baptist, asked who do you say?
Of the would-be penitents who crowded his
        way,
But bowed in awe before the Nazarene, his
        cousin
Made a speech, as well as a bit of a scene.

And the climactic word of poetry spoken
By that prophet, alias lion, also known as lamb,
Throwing Judas and cohorts to the ground,
Was the natural reply, "I am."

GRAVE ROBBER

He was not normal, as most of us might expect,
Seeing what he did, that inclination of his,
Early noted, to extreme disrespect.

Even his friends cite a number of signs
That he was a "sport," unfortunate aberrant
Who responded to rules by crossing the lines.

The home-town people, who would have
        known him best,
Showed great reserve when he visited them
And nodded their heads when he failed the
        test.

For his mother was young when he came and
        unstable,
His stepfather (both said he was that) old and
        soon dead
And several other children around the table.

Conceived out of wedlock, oldest of the crew,
Early given responsibility, under mother's
        sway,
It's a wonder he didn't do murder, too.

So when he claimed to be one who "saves, "
Hypnotizing hundreds, cursing temple stones,
We should have known he'd end robbing
        graves,
Desecrating tombs -- even his own.

OPEN-EYED PRAYERS

It is no new issue, this meal-time skirmish
Over postures and principles of prayer:
Hands -- to hold or to fold;
How much stillness required;
Do we take turns or should Dad lead;
Memorized or inspired?
But the conflict most frequent, the best
       question posed
Has to do with eyes: open or closed?

For faith and vision are not easily joined,
The canonical formula poses the tension
Faith - "the evidence of things unseen"
Goes well with "I was the last to open my eyes
When we prayed," my youngest's proud claim
-- Difficult to discount or despise.
And is there a point, if ironically made,
In "Adriel opened her eyes when we prayed"?

The conundrum is not one soon unknotted,
But these things we know, these we see:
Faith and vision converge, though they differ;
Though eyes dim, hearts' eyes grow sharp;
Seeing others' seeing is not eyes' function;
Faith may seize the day while eyes carp,
And see the past and the future as one,
Praying with eyes wide, "Thy will be done".

NO LOVE WORTH HAVING

No love worth having is worth having first:
First, erratic, sheer love is the worst.
Love disappointed, love disillusioned
Is love grown sober, refined by confusion.

No love worth having is innocent, whole,
Unalloyed, untouched by any love other.
Such a love is worship, its object's role
That of a god, not a mortal brother.

Seek a woman's love, not her first, but her
     second.
Answer no siren no other has beckoned:
Make sure her ardor knows another altar;
For single, all-consuming love will falter
And fall burnt out, consumed, despised.

No love worth having hasn't first loved Christ.

PARABOLIC

You expect me to believe this! To take
     seriously your pledge
For food, drink, whatever this accident
     victim of yours might need?
I heard your story, he was attacked, you
     found him under a hedge,
But he's no kin to you! Well, I've family to
     clothe and feed
And I never yet found their bellies content

on alms I spent.

You're a foreigner aren't you, one of that
        troublesome bunch
Over the border. No one else would, you
        say, but then why you?
All right, I see your coin is good and. . . I
        admit I have a hunch
You really mean to pay for all his care, I
        don't know why I do
Unless it's what you've so far done, deeds so
        rare under the sun.

You'll make up anything over? I heard you
        right? You know
That could include damages, loss of life,
        health, respect
And business -- Lord, what might happen
        with one found so --
You'll pay all and above? All right I'll do it -
        - despite your sect.
It's a comfort to know you're not shy where
        others pass by.

THE FAIREST IS THE BROWN

Oh the golden she is noble and the silver she is
        fair
And where they're found, well I'll be bound
Good things aren't wanting there,
But I have found best riches in country or in
        town

Among the poor and lowly,
The fairest is the brown.

Kings crowns, eagles bright, coins heavy in the
    hand
Are money the world over, are ships come to
    land;
But nobles' chests and bankers vests
Though they hold so many a pound
Do not compare, be they ever so fair
With the humble little brown.

For the deep ring that the gold coins sing
And the tolling of silver streams
Rings hollow here and in God's ear, by the tale
    told 'twould seem.
The high king's heart did fairly start when last
    he was in town
To hear the still small chime rung,
By that fairest little brown.

YOU DON'T WANT TO MARRY SOMEONE LIKE YOUR MOTHER

You don't want to marry someone like your
    mother –
But you always do. We are forever trying the
    same foot
 On the other shoe. There are really very few
    new things
Under the sun. And wives and mothers --
    aren't one.

I suppose a fatalist, a hard core stoic might
      find pleasure
Of a perverse sort in the expectation that makes a
      romantic optimist
Like me frantic -- that what you just escaped in
      fates
Waits around the corner of the next block,
      second installment.

You don't want to marry someone like your ex-
      wife,
But you always do. Have you ever suspected
      there might be
Something in your luggage or lurking behind
      each bush --
That old childhood nightmare there to give
      you another fright?

You don't want a boss like your old Dad -- do
      you?
But he always is. It's almost like voodoo how
      it goes
With the territory -- your territory I mean. He
      pushes
Or doesn't push you exactly like you do or
      don't want pushing.

You don't want children like your parents,
      spouse,
Not in your house! No grinners, gripers,
      growlers,
No lazy, driven, sloppy, no bright, dull,

drunken, sober,
Ignoramuses just exactly like those other ones
    you hate.

But there they are. Do you wonder how they
    got there?

HUNGER PANGS

Hunger pangs (I've been enlightened, now
    know)
Are not pains of the stomach, achings from the
    void,
But signals, false but true signals,
From one endocrine gland or the other
Based on blood-sugar levels, telling you to eat!

In diabolical experiments the fact has been
    proven
By stimulating helpless rats by appropriate
    means
To eat themselves to death,
Or conversely to starve, without a pang of
    hunger.

And these pangs of soul, these hollow-heart
    hurts --
Might they be likewise, some gland of spirit
Signaling us we wander desperate straits,
And need to hurry on Home to supper?

THE MUSES

Those Muses whom we humourously invoke
Or not so humourously;
Who give, we are told,
Their favored few true inspiration,
Are heathen goddesses:
They own no creed, no code,
Nor care for those they visit --
Except as playthings.
Their long-sought visions
Once received are awful things,
Casting those possessed by them
Into water and into fire.
Saint Paul warns seekers of Muses:
That the gods of the heathen are demons;
The things which the Gentiles sacrifice,
They sacrifice unto devils.

DEDICATION

Roseann, gracious rose,
Odor of life to God and me,
Sweet climber upon the rock,
Encircler free:
Artful artless bloom thou art;
None attains thy moderate height,
Nor Christ clean, shines as white.

Mother of love,
Author of truth,
Roseann, thou hast been to me;
Innocent tempter toward love and truth set in
Eternity.

Miller of meals,
Iron armed,
Laver of children,
Lawyer, clerk;
Editor, critic, teacher,
Roseann: of Christ the work.

Taken my name, leaving thine,
Roseann, how grown this little of mine;
Oh, wife, dear lover, sister free,
This little take from my poor pen,
True gift, as Christ rose, for me.

THE UNDERTAKERS

The undertakers of this world get last respects,
Coming somewhere after garbagemen in
      preferment.
They are supposed to be cold hypocritical
      beings,
Stealing pennies from the world's eyelids.

I know but few and therefore must be excused
For thinking perhaps they are truest artists.
Some I've found to be fully as human
As any poet, painter, or composer.

They have this one advantage over all,
(Not counting the well-known fact
They will have the last word)
They know without a doubt
The moment for which they labor.
Their crafts, mechanical and awful
Are undertaken with conscious mortality:
Aimed toward the funeral, that brief half-hour
When, framed as well as economy allows,
The finished work is placed on exhibition.
The time completed, the curtains drawn,
The lid lowered, that work is done:
Gone on to dust as will all works,
Gone, I'm afraid, to corruption.
Many attending are edified or think they are,
Certainly as much by undertakers' as by much
Wiggling work of teeming artists.
My conclusion: undertakers are less
         hypocrites than we
Who do not know our work is dead:
Who white the tomb not knowing it such,
Being too fastidious to deal with bodies.

GOOD FRIDAY ON THE ROAD

My road dips through the woods,
Sun low behind the trees,
Where welts of tree shadow shudder my
         vision.
Eyes blink in cosmic winking,
But are not drawn from the road.
The static of tree shadows interrupts my

narrow journey.
Each successive shade flicks front and back,
Mocking me with a sense of spinning
But I must go the whole way.
The vibrato of tree shadows rings psyche
      deep,
Like strokes of iron sharpening sense.
The stroboscopic mesmerists, tree shutters
Fail to spawn a trance, to pickle my mind
Toward almost obliging oblivion.
The road curving under tree shadows remains
      my road
Upon which I must continue
No matter how excruciating to eyes of weary
      flesh,
This Good Friday on the road.

MOCKERY IN THE MORNING

The   bird   which   awakens   us
Every   morning   just past the thief's hour
Does not mock us in the ordinary sense.
His cheerful, starkly exuberant songs
Involve no duplicity on his part,
No intention toward parody or satire.
Although the hour and volume
As they echo down the street
Are more than we'd tolerate from any other
      neighbor,
None of us grumbles or grudges lost sleep.
The mockingbird matins are beyond
      blaspheming

Our sorrow, our dreary bed-borne groaning.
They humiliate us out of troubled earthly
      dreams --
Roll the stones from hearts in blessed
      mockery.

FOOD AND CLOTHING

Take eat cracked the voice of the Kraken
See your fellowship broken, be gods --
      forsaken
Himself by the spirit who moved on the
      waters
And in the soul of this first of his daughters.

Take eat crooned Eve, sticky-mouthed
      seducer,
Sin's sweet, taste and see, the best for you, sir.
Stripped barer than her skin, her claim
To feed her husband was to clothe her blame.

Who told you you were unclothed and naked,
My spirit heart breaks, you have been snaked
By the arch-light, arch-cook, would be
      monarch
Himself stripped and starved of me, long
      dark.

Go and hunger, pain to bear, sweat to bake
More mouths to feed, more garments to make,
Naked heads, naked heels will ever contend
Until I bring food and clothing to mend.

Take eat said the serpent, like God be clothed.
Take eat, said Eve. Leaf aprons they sewed
Eat bread, said God, now in bloody hides
    dress.

"Take eat" Christ said, wear my righteousness.

'TIS A PITY

Don't pity me.
I cannot stand the piteous glance
Or pity-ful hand which reached out
From a heart of pity.
Don't pity me.

It's a pitiful thing
For men to be so smug, so grand
In their sweet pity. Sweet to them!
But bitter to us.
A pitiful thing.

Not pity they think,
Serendipity! What luck for you!
We happened to see your desperate need.
Ha! luck indeed!
It's pity all right.

Useless pity,
It cannot heal my real hurt --
The way I feel, my aching heart,
My need for love.

Useless pity.

Does pity go back
To sumptious home and roaring fire
Leaving me alone and desperate yet
More desperate for love?
Damn such pity.

Effectual pity!
You know my need! Your head is bowed
Your hands bleed and your eyes descend
To sweep up my sin.
Yes, this is pity that takes me in.

WIND-SHAKEN REED

A reed shaken by the wind
Was never the object of my wilderness
      seeking,
(Even desert dwellers wander near water)
Was never a goal,
But always a companion like the reed-shaking
      wind.

Cattail, bulrush, snakegrass, reed
Quivering before the relentless force
Of unseen reality, the contrast
Between thin, soon brittle self
And what eternally rises up again.

Reeds feed locusts and wild bees.
Rather than seek to be sought,

Tremble at the enormity of the task,
To not only pull the shoestrings of the wind,
But pour out chrism on its head.

OX AND ASS

God blew life into Adam, that cud of mud,
Made in his image.
Did some mysterious sigh fill the creatures,
    too?

What blinking bashfulness must then have
    come
Upon the witnesses to his first --
The ox and ass puffing warm straw breaths
Some small return of what invests.

As light through glass the spirit came
Upon the virgin first,
But ancient curse brought forth old pain
When out the god-child burst.

He breathed those gathered breaths back in
And firmamental lungs sucked sin.

Gentle ox and ass shared air with I am --
May they not breathe easy with lion and
    lamb?

James Howard Trott

MOCKINGBIRD BEFORE DAWN

In the strait bonds of not-yet dawn
The mockingbird is mad with an
    unmistakable note,
Declares he's not quite sure what
With ridiculous zeal.

There is a denotation to his wordless pledge,
A finer-tuned declaration in his garbled
    gargle.
It is not just association
Makes me say.

Listen yourself: Hear the heart of him
Rush up his throat past his little brain
And pour out the mystery of his entrails --
It will be morning.

POETIC MADNESS

If poetry is madness,
Cracked cants in verse,
Its devotees wine-drunk,
Hydro-phobic, or worse,
One ought to be cautious,
As in marriage or trade,
Have a healthy respect,
Even be afraid:
Know the mad-making poet,
Know his foam-signed bites,
Know he spreads the madness

Through the words he writes.

IMMIGRANTS

Immigrants wailed heartstruck about their
    shacks.
We murdered their children,
Tore apart their makeshift homes
And threw down the bare, helpless things,
Breaking then scarcely from the womb.
We pursued foreigners in fancy dress,
Laughed at each wild-eyed, long-legged
    dodger,
Shooting them when we could.
Sometimes when the river was low
We'd steal along the backwater banks
Where other late-comers swam,
And beat their struggling backs with clubs
Or dragged them gasping from the shallow
    mud.

There was also some fighting among the
    natives,
But only the foreigners, ill-kempt, unclean,
With their senseless gabble,
Or ludicrous in heathen dress
Were fools enough to be so vulnerable.
They got full brunt of our brutality.
Sparrows, pheasants, and carp
Were strangers and aliens, wanderers
In the place once my home.

DEFENSIVE

If a workman defends his handiwork,
Or a mother her child, full well
Though both may know them wrong;
Why such surprise at the ancient song
Priests and prophets tell,
God gave himself for godless man
And defended him down to hell.

IN THE CLEFT OF THE ROCK

I barely know God's smooth back.
Still crouched in this narrow way,
I cower down among the alpine flowers,
Which blossom like Aaron's rod
And stand so still, whisper ecstasy
In my hands blind embrace
Of what I most fear and long for --
End of guilt, garden innocence,
And long sight of the bridegroom's face.

IN THE SAME ROOM

Grandfather and I ganged up and attacked the
    middle generation,
The stricken go-betweens who crossed our
    worlds in the same room.

He cried because of lies a president spoke
    bravely publicly,
Before the war to end all wars, saying our

young men would never go.

He cried because our young men went, and his
    eldest son died.
I saw all the others struck dumb, some of
    whom had gone to war, too.

Years later I disabled them again with tears,
    cried out of ideals,
Cried at a promise no one ever spoke that
    parents always know,
Always understand and always respond to
    what one knows and feels.

I cried at awareness creeping up on me: I was
    born of mortals.
Between us they were helpless; caught under
    converging tears
In the same room.

NEMATODES

With a twinkling eye and a voice of glee
(There is joy in every truth)
Professor Levi told a squirming class
About a hypothetical proof
For nematodes ubiquity
Amidst earth's living mass.

Were organic matter to disappear
To melt away like snow in the sun --
Except for the earnest nematode,

(He did not say how it might be done)
All men, animals and plants here
Would still be shadowed.

Groans arose as awareness dawned
Of what our crawling flesh had spawned,
What cities spread over soaped skin,
What myriad hoards all housed within.
Shivers ran up learned backs,
Nematode earthquakes, over simple facts.

Many Manichaeans were born that day.
Confirmed Epicureans left to go drinking.
How to man a city so thoroughly wormed,
Some few Stoics fell to thinking --
That we were less pure than the other way
Was for most that day confirmed.

I sing nematodes and the man, still --
Homo condominium -- to death I will.
Doing battle yet with the worms in my
        brain,
I ponder a marvel -- what shadow of gain
For the vermin-free one who entered in
To teeming flesh to exterminate sin?

A ROOFER'S PRAYER

Some men work with marble,
Some men work with gold,
But plain slate and copper
Are the best I ever hold.

Up on the ridgepole,
I watch the world and weather,
Lay my lines and shingles
Wearing out cloth and leather.

I feel the cold, I feel the heat,
I see the storm clouds come,
I feel time aching in my bones
When my long day's work is done.

I smell spring the day it comes,
Taste fall before leaves burn,
I see the birds arrive and adieu,
Hear the wild geese call and turn.

I hold nails in the palm of my hands,
Know the hell of an August sun,
My work serves a purpose,
Rain proves what I have done.

Someday all men's work will end,
The weary world will stop,
And what men have and have not done
Will ring from some rooftop.

A ladder that only one Man could lift
Will extend to eternity's eaves,
And those on the rooftops will not come
    down
To share what the groundman receives.

Or someday I'll drop from this ladder,

Lord prevent I do --
Or Jesus with your calloused hands
Then raise me up with you.

TOOKANY CREEK

City-bound plastic-spotted rubber-tired
      stream,
What remnants of a mystical essence
Can you have?
The vendors of soft-pretzels on the islands
Of the avenues
Hold their questionable wares high --
      advertise them.

Won't you learn?

In the early morning light I saw a plane,
Should have been a plane of smooth light,
But for the surface-breaking rocks,
And the dying tendency to run down.

At evening I returned along the road
Of joggers and plastic-buggied duffers
Where I saw the antsy day caught, locked
In Tookany Creek's deep amber.

And now the winter freezes even the waves
Breaking over hidden stone, until the thaw of
      spring.

A LIFE IN THE DAY - GREEN CREEK

It's hard to know, it's difficult
And weighs on one wondering
If the rooster crows merely from habit
Or in genuine amazement at the dawn.

One would add exuberance at the prospect of
     a new day,
But exuberance is the sort of pathetic fallacy
Promoted by fatuous romanticism and
Doubtful usage, even when used of humans.
Nor is all romanticism fatuous.
But the sun strikes level across the world
And fronts the brazen rooster yet more
     brazenly,
So I suspect it's amazement.

You can't get away from dawn.
Down in the drip-rich ferns,
The toads which went a-hopping all night long
Are hiding, but not ignoring it.
You might say their obfuscation
Was a matter of deep respect.
They know light when they see it,
And find it frightening enough
To come out just before dusk to migrate
Somewhat purposefully toward a purpose,
Which they need not know to make it signify.

And the bat that ran the airy rodent trails
Through the tree tops on winged feet
Is also cloistered now,

Musing its upside-down dreams
Of tasty Lepidoptera metamorphosing
Up in the chrysalis of its intestines.
One sleeps as another rises.
A death for a birth, a new life for an old.

When we got up, we squelched anticipation.
That is a habit --
Perhaps "good morning" more than the cock's
        cough.
We forbore hoping overmuch or fearing,
And vaguely looked for breakfast,
Which is hardly fair if fasting is for prayer.
Only the very holy pray in their sleep,
And dreams, like sleep come willy-nilly,
Seldom, themselves, prayers,
Unless prayers of repentance yet to be
        repented,
Or of hopes yet to be admitted.
So the fast is an enforced one with little fruit,
Call it what you will.

Then we begin to plan, or rather
Remember fragments large and small of plans,
And put together a montage of an itinerary,

Which suddenly we're in the midst of
With only so much as a howdy-do
We begin to work which may turn out our
        salvation yet,
Since it is such a certain link
To what our crew knew before the cock.
Work beats down the body and squeezes out

the old man
Who cannot stand it, except as an escape
From something he fears more.
That, too, enters into our work, the best of it
-- The fact our mind and hands are set upon
    a task,
A seen task which probably can be
    completed,
Rather than an unseen one to which all the
    indications
Thoroughly deny conclusion.
Yet work will even refine that,
Given world enough and time.

We eat again -- near the peak of light
The zenith of our relatively spinning sky
To the stable sun we cannot help but
Caricature as moving, rising, setting.
We eat and our longing stomachs find
It wholesomely satisfactory to taste
Preliminary bread out of preliminary sweat.
There is a definite promise there
Of indefinite rewards and labor.
But not much rest -- work continues,
The harder for the full stomach,
And the disappointed sense we've done
    enough
-- Why must this go on?

The peak of heat comes then,
After the horizon has begun to climb,
Earth saturated with absorbed light,
Not comprehending it, but using it

To radiate in the face of the sun.
We are caught between, or among --
The hot earth, the sun and our tasks,
And almost despair, but put that off, too,
On the outside chance something's afoot.

When evening comes, though the cock's
    comb droop,
We gather back to table and pitcher,
Confident something is finished for sure,
Something is irrevocably closed,
Never to be brought against us again,
And the chickens bunch going in to roost,
While mosquitoes emerge for a last
    irritation,
Before we go blessedly to bed,
And the toad hops,
And bat wends,
And the rooster goes to sleep all
    unsuspecting.

TO EVE

I see Eve sensuous and supple,
What strange creature is this
Who stirs my blood in such new ways.
This is the best of creatures, Maker.

I see Eve sinuous and sighing,
What powerful creature is this
Who reins my will with such force,
This most awful of creatures.

I still see Eve and see double,
Two eyes, two breasts -- two masters --
Split commitments, divided loyalties,
Eve the upright, and the crossbeam Eve.

NO MAN'S LAND
(John 8)

No man stands, no man can
No man ban's another's sins
   -- in no man's land.

No unknowns, no one owns,
No one stones no one's bones
   -- in no man's land.

Sinners must, sinners trust,
Fingers drawing in their dust
   -- in no man's land.

Strokes fell, wounds tell,
Forgiveness bore some others' hell:
One man -- in no man's land.

STIGMATUM

Albert Calkin got one in high school
When he reached into a bailer
And the tying arm went through his palm,
Leaving a big white scar --

Bailing hay, binding up
Both grain and straw for the future.

Dave Dyrland got one in the army
Two weeks before his tour was up
Flying in a Chinook air-lifting water.
The Viet Cong shell pierced a wire cable,
And an empty ammo can before lodging in his
     cheek,
It knocked him down but he got back up.

My wife has had two, right on top of each
     other,
C- sections, Caesarean deliveries,
And hers, like His, not only dripped blood,
But brought forth living children.

NO MILESTONE

So he walked
(At first he had jogged)
Into the gathering
Thickening fog.
He'd expected decay
To come crack by crack,
Or with limbs failing
All at a whack.
But these obscured powers,
This twilight zone,
Was beyond what he reckoned.
There was no milestone.

ONE CANDLE IN A ROOM

One candle in a room: one place, one light.
Two candles in a room cast shadows but half
    night.
A light bulb, a chandelier dispel some surface
    gloom,
But nothing lights better than one candle in a
    room.

There is nothing clearer than one candle in a
    place,
Casting honest shadows across bare wall and
    face,
Lighting honest glimmers in eyes and glass,
Delineating what remains and what flickers
    past.

One candle in a room burns steadily in calm
Or leaps and neaps before a draft like man in a
    psalm,
Pouring out two sincere streams as 'round it
    shadows loom.
And at its foot, substantial blood -- one candle
    in a room.

CITY STORM

. . .The cars full of people
Used to thriving on the first
Thirty seconds of romance

Now grimace with dampened enthusiasm
Behind wailing wipers. . .

. . .The drops etched leopard spots
On the street's skin
Sliding across asphalt muscles
Beneath the fractured lights. . .

. . .A staring stalker
Of the endless streets stops,
Listening for a moment to the wind
Knocking his pants' legs' knees. . .

. . .The freight-yards of heaven
Boom and clash with traffic
Of ominous cargos coupling together
For a long night train. . .

. . .In this near paradise
Where one must learn
To be vigilant against the snake
It is refreshing to look upward for trouble. . .

GROTESQUERIES OF WINTER

Bleak, this frozen, barren earth,
Stone-marked, heaped with detritus of death,
Hopeless if hope has meaning here,
With no relief, unless the threadbare pall
Of snow be called relief -- only cover.
When I remember past fertile beauty . . .
But here upon this stone, a tuft of living moss.

Awful, these hulking dead grotesqueries
With twisted, stained, and somber arms
Reaching unanswered to the sky,
Holding to earth with rigorous grips
Like desperate clawed corpses.
Surely life is lost to these . . .
Is that a bud?

FINAL EXAMINATIONS

It's hard that people need you so little when
   they're gone.
There's little consideration when they go --
For us who labored for them so much when
   they were here,
Or planned to -- how can they leave us so?

It's not only that we miss them, though that's
   bad, bad enough,
It's not only all the stir their partings bring
Nor just the space they used to fill -- so hard to
   fill again,
But the way it seems so final that's the thing.

For they take tomorrow's cookies - no one will
   ever bake.
They take next Easter's flowers with them, too.
They take the little jokes we've saved and
   newsy scraps of news
Along with other things we'll never do.

And though we had forgotten for a while to
      call or write,
Didn't drop by the house or visit in their room
In so many months we're just a little bit
      ashamed,
All at once they're things we never can resume.

It's hard how little people seem to need you
      when they're gone,
How little they consider when they fly
Us who thought of laboring so much on their
      behalf,
While they thought no more of us than to die.

THE LADDER

Yes, men throw grappling hooks, scale ropes,
Stand tiptoe atop stools and reach,
How they, how we reach,
But any who make a livelihood of climbing
Require a ladder, rungs and rails.

Rungs, those sturdy rounds run horizontal.
Each man moves upon relationships
To mother, father, wife, child, friend.

Rails, the spanning beams from earth to heaven
Support the rungs and give what continuity
There is to climbing.

Rungs without rails are kindling,
Rails without rungs but poles.

Love the Lord, ah, yes,
And love your neighbor.

THE WILD GEESE

I. GOOSE CALLS

Three weeks of geese this unstable November,
Taught me all I know again,
Re-gummed the well-used stamps
That license my earth letters.
Three weeks of weather rough and mild,
With geese the only constant,
Their morning flights from field beds,
Their wide return at evening.
Where have they been these days?
Whence have they been coming?
My natural history comes up short --
I cannot say.
I guess they fly to water.
Their purposes here, in such numbers,
Must mean they gather,
Gather and together gain
Strength, and order,
The common will to make the flight
To mystical places of their wintering.
We, too, muster for the winter,
We watch and hearken, grow ready with them,
Feeding and sailing out and in,
On different wings, but similar thoughts,
As we ponder the wild geese again,

Trying to make some normal
From the calls that startle their own longing.

II. ARRIVAL

The adolescent voices of the wild geese
       breaking
Break our Autumn hearts afar.
We hear them some before we see them,
See them go, but cannot reach
The limber-winged sky-swimmers,
Beating substance into this word beyond --
The beyond from which they come,
That beyond to which they go.
These morning signs beckon us,
Ethereal bodies white and shining
On wings dark with shades of meaning.
The geese sound the note of my watchdog
       heart
Barking at those strangers,
And alerting that poor master mind.

III. AUTUMN ACRONYMS

The geese call up lump-throat backchills,
In the whispery autumn,
Unseen until we strain our sight
To read the fine-traced pointillation
In the sky, the high sky,
Above the world's effluence.

There they trace the gnomic signs
Their mysteries heart-breaking:
"V" for voices
"Y" for youth

"L" for love
Or a "J" askew.

Semaphore wings flashing light,
Splashing flashes from their broad wings,
Signal some urgent message.

Our hearts long for the north, they say,
Where the wild winds suit our songs,
But we are too weak, too wise to stay
Where the winter howls so long.

Or do they say that?
This year I seem to have grown near-sighted,
Too near-sighted to read.

IV.   THE MORNING FLIGHT
The sky portraits in white, gray and black:
At early morning, lit from below,
Morning Sun lights their white bellies
            innocent.
Their necks and beaks are black. . . gray wings
(Lo, if I take the wings of the morning ...)
But as the sun climbs, true colors appear,
Tails white (loins girt about with truth),
Bellies, gray, and air-ruling wings black.
Then going to the sun, they grow darker
Until disappeared in the blinding south-maker.

V. THE EVENING RETURN
Great strings breaking and separating,
Crossing and meeting, fusing, fleeing,

Hurtling, wheeling, formations within
        formations,
Rushing up and spreading like waves on a
        shore,
Turning, receding,
And always the calling, each to each,
The broken call of the almost departed.
Rising, falling lines descend,
Jerk my puppet-stringed heart.

Which is leader? They shift and peel.
Back falls the foremost,
Up a new pioneer to take the cutting wind
On her beak and breast,
Until she, too, needs follow others.

As a line of five, too few to "V"
Sweep over the trees, the leftmost veers,
Deciding who knows what, diverges,
Parts, and starts on his own way,
While the right-hand goose pulls his.
But those in the middle,
Diffuse between them, cry the two,
Call for peace, desiring unity more than either,
Pull them gently back together.

The single geese are few, pass briefly,
        sometimes stranded
When a large "V" splits, unable to choose,
The straggler wavers, remains between.
But a lone goose cannot keep silent
Though none flies beside or hears.
Considering himself an outrider

For those he cannot see
He calls out and labors on.

Two gaggles fly opposed paths, approach.
They shift directions until their roads,
And their diverse formations merge
Into a single phalanx.

From afar the strings of dot-bodies,
Connected by wing-dashes seem some code,
Writ small to worry a cryptographer.

Corpuscles of wanderlust, diffusing and
       clotting
Pass among the bare branches
Among the oak leaves, dead though clinging,
Scatter like shot from behind the tops of
       winter pines.

VI. A WINTER EVENING CLOSES

The motor cycle gangs of somber clouds
Were not softer for the rosy tinge,
Brief sunset passengers among them.
They sped across the sky almost as relentless
As the wounding wild geese
With sunset-bloodied breasts,
Flying crosses, phalanxes of darts,
With fingerless hands, reaching, reaching,
With churning joints in hollow bone
Borne on hollow feathers beating
Out the winnow-weather skirr,
Driving on the chaff of days.
The relentless surge of martial pinions

Whistles softly, on, on. . .
Subtly, shrilly, pipe away,
Always on and away.

VII. THE WILD GEESE AGAIN

They come, they go these brief interminable
        days,
Blending their calls with harsh wet winds,
And the stillness of frost-breaking sunshine.
Their passing shivers in us,
But their waiting to go throbs, aches deeper,
The inscrutability of their essence,
Their existence, their ideals,
Drives the mind to stoically ignoring
The plaintive cries of their altruism.
Wings scrawl alternate smiles and frowns,
Raised eyebrows and bowed backs blend
Against the blue and gray,
But now their formations are tighter,
Their purpose grows more single.

VIII. ADIEU

The last evening before Thanksgiving day
I saw (adieu) a long last "V"
Over the sunset wood fringe,
Kindled but not consumed.
The dying sun lit red wing beacons
To signal their departure.
What is this strange melancholy
That sets my heart beating --
Which has me aching to go with them
. . . Or is it an " r " promising their return?

APPENDIX – POEMS PREVIOUSLY PUBLISHED IN PERIODICALS:

"AT THE NURSING HOME" – *Cornerstone* , 1991.

"BETWEEN APRIL FOOLS' AND EASTER" – *Christianity and Literature*,Vol. XXXIII No. 2, Winter 1984, p. 30.

"BOBBY" - *New Horizons*, Vol. 6, No. 4, April 1985, page 18; and a different version in *Time of Singing*, Vol XIII, Number 3, September 1986, p. 14.

"BROKER" - *The Banner*, Vol 127, No.34, October 5, 1992.

"A DECIDED LACK OF DECORUM" – *Cornerstone*, Vol 14, issue 7? (summer 1985), p. 24.

"DEFENSIVE" – *The Banner* , Vol 127, No. 31, September 30, 1991, p. 3.

"DEMANDS, DESIRES, WANTS, NEEDS" - *Cornerstone Magazine*, Vol. 12, issue 67, (l983), p. 11.

"ELUSIVITY" - *SYMPHONY*, 1987, No. 1, p.19.

"FASTENERS" - *The Banner*, Vol 121, No. 6, February 17, 1986, p. 4.

"FOUR EGGS" - *Christianity and Literature*, Vol. XXXII, No. 3, Spring 1983, p. 30.

"IMMINENCE" - *Wellspring* , volume five, number three/four (July-December, 1983).

"IN MEMORY OF ISABEL JOHNS" - *Cornerstone*, Vol 18, Iss. 89 (Sep 89), p. 25.

"LIKE A LOVER'S LOVE" - *Plains Poetry Journal*, No. 30, July 1989, p. 10.

"METAPHYSICS" - *Chronicles*, accepted Aug 1988.

"MOCKERY IN THE MORNING" - Time of Singing, Volume XIV, Number 2, April 1987, p. 33.

"MOONLIGHT" (from "The Big Lights", *New Hope International*, Hyde,   England, published on p. 26, Vol. 13, No. 6 1989/90; (from poem cycle, "THE BIG LIGHTS" also published by *New Hope International*, 1989, as a chapbook, cover illustration by James Edwards Trott.)

"MY HANDS" – *The Banner*, Vol 128, No. 42, December 6, 1993, p. 11.

"NO LOVE WORTH HAVING" – *The Banner*, Vol 128, No. 27, August 9, 1993.

"NO MAN'S LAND" - *The Banner*, Vol 122, No. 27, July 27, 1987, p. 13.

"OF POTS AND POETS" - "Porch Swing Rhyme," poetry column of The Society of Christian Poets, Van Buren, Arkansas; July 12, 1984.

"RAIN WITH WIND" – *Cornerstone*, Vol l0, issue 59, March/April (l982), p. 24.

"REACH ME" - Accepted by *The Banner*, March 1993, pub date unknown.

"ROUGH ROADS" - *Symphony*, November 1985, (England)

"SALOME" - accepted (Jan 87) by *New Hope International*, Hyde, England, pub date unknown.

"SINGING ON THEIR KNEES" - *Plains Poetry Journal*, Number Twenty-seven, October 1988, p.41.

"TAXES" - *Cornerstone*, Vol. 16, issue 84, (winter 1987), p.30.

"THIS LITTLE LIGHT OF MINE" – *Cornerstone*, Vol. 13, issue 70, (summer 1984).

"THOU SAYEST" - *Symphony*, November 1985, (England).

"'TIS A PITY" - *Cornerstone*, May 89 or early 199 .

"TO A CHILD LEARNING TO DIVE" – *Cornerstone*, 1991.

"TO LEAVE MY DAUGHTER IN HER DISTANT ROOM IS PAINFUL" – *Cornerstone*, Vol 14, Issue 76 (December 1985), p. 32.

"TO A SNAKE ON THE ROCK IN OUR PASTURE" – *Cornerstone*, Vol 13, issue 70 (summer 1984); different version in *Time of Singing*, Volume XI, Number 2, (August 1984), p. 24.

"TWO LOVERS" - *Cornerstone*, Vol 15, Issue 79, Summer 1986, (p. 24).

"URIAH" - Accepted *Chronicles* - Aug 1988 , pub date unknown, possibly not published.

"THE WASTING OF OUR POWERS" – *Cornerstone*, Vol 19, Issue 92, Summer 1990, p. 25.

"WEAPONRY" - *Banner* – pub date unknown.

www.ingramcontent.com/pod-product-compliance
Lightning Source LLC
Chambersburg PA
CBHW061954070426
42450CB00011BA/2817